MARK AQUINO RN

NCLEX RN Review Simplified

An NCLEX Review Study Guide Organized by Systems – Just the Essentials With Sample Questions

Copyright © 2023 by Mark Aquino RN

All rights reserved. No part of this publication may be reproduced, stored or transmitted in any form or by any means, electronic, mechanical, photocopying, recording, scanning, or otherwise without written permission from the publisher. It is illegal to copy this book, post it to a website, or distribute it by any other means without permission.

Mark Aquino RN has no responsibility for the persistence or accuracy of URLs for external or third-party Internet Websites referred to in this publication and does not guarantee that any content on such Websites is, or will remain, accurate or appropriate.

Designations used by companies to distinguish their products are often claimed as trademarks. All brand names and product names used in this book and on its cover are trade names, service marks, trademarks and registered trademarks of their respective owners. The publishers and the book are not associated with any product or vendor mentioned in this book. None of the companies referenced within the book have endorsed the book.

By reading this material or the documents it offers, you assume all risks associated with using the advice given, with a full understanding that you, solely, are responsible for anything that may occur as a result of putting this information into action in any way, and regardless of your interpretation of the advice.

The medical information in this book is not advice and should not be treated as such. Do not substitute this information for the medical advice of physicians. The information is general and intended to better inform readers of their health care. Always consult your doctor for your individual needs. Consult a physician for matters relating to your health and any symptoms that may require diagnosis or medical attention.

The author of this book disclaims liability for any loss or damage suffered by any person as a result of the information or content in this book. The information in this book is for educational purposes only.

First edition

This book was professionally typeset on Reedsy.
Find out more at reedsy.com

Contents

Preface	xiii
FREE EBOOK: Sign Up for the FREE Nurse's Quickstart Kit!	xiii
"NCLEX RN Review Simplified: An NCLEX Review Study Guide Organized by Systems – Just the Essentials with Sample Questions"	xv
FREE EBOOK: Sign Up for the FREE Nurse's Quickstart Kit!	xix
Acknowledgement	xx
1 Nursing Fundamentals	1
Environmental Safety and Emergency Preparedness	5
Admission and Discharge Planning	6
Patient Education Principles	6
Communication Skills in Nursing	7
Documentation and Charting	7
Delegation and Supervision in Nursing	8
Ethical and Legal Considerations in Nursing	8
End-of-Life Care and Palliative Care	9
Advanced Directives and Living Wills	10
Therapeutic Diets and Nutrition Support	10
Pain Assessment Tools	11
Non-Pharmacological Pain Management	12
Therapeutic Communication Techniques	12
Cultural Competency in Nursing Care	13
Health Disparities and Social Determinants of Health	13
Health Promotion and Disease Prevention	14
Nursing Process: Assessment, Diagnosis, Planning, Implementation, Evaluation	15

Vital Signs Monitoring	15
Fluid and Electrolyte Balance	16
Acid-Base Balance	16
Aseptic Technique and Sterile Procedures	17
Oxygenation and Ventilation	18
Basic Life Support (BLS) and Cardiopulmonary Resuscitation (CPR)	18
2 Adult Medical-Surgical Nursing Part 1	20
Cardiovascular System Disorders	20
Coronary Artery Disease (CAD)	20
Hypertension (High Blood Pressure)	21
Heart Failure	21
Arrhythmias (e.g., Atrial Fibrillation)	22
Cardiomyopathies	23
Peripheral Artery Disease (PAD)	23
Valvular Heart Diseases (e.g., Mitral Valve Prolapse)	24
Congenital Heart Diseases	25
Deep Vein Thrombosis (DVT) and Pulmonary Embolism	25
Aortic Aneurysms	26
Respiratory System Disorders	26
Asthma	27
Chronic Obstructive Pulmonary Disease (COPD)	27
Pneumonia	28
Pulmonary Embolism	29
Tuberculosis	29
Lung Cancer	30
Pulmonary Hypertension	31
Cystic Fibrosis	31
Pleural Effusion	32
Sleep Apnea	32
Gastrointestinal System Disorders	33
Gastroesophageal Reflux Disease (GERD)	33
Peptic Ulcers	34

Crohn's Disease	34
Ulcerative Colitis	35
Irritable Bowel Syndrome (IBS)	36
Gallstones	36
Hepatitis	37
Pancreatitis	38
Gastroenteritis	38
Colorectal Cancer	39
Neurological System Disorders	39
Stroke	40
Alzheimer's Disease	40
Parkinson's Disease	41
Multiple Sclerosis	42
Epilepsy	42
Migraines and Other Types of Headaches	43
Amyotrophic Lateral Sclerosis (ALS)	44
Meningitis	44
Peripheral Neuropathy	45
Traumatic Brain Injury (TBI)	46
Musculoskeletal System Disorders	46
Osteoarthritis	46
Rheumatoid Arthritis	47
Osteoporosis	48
Gout	48
Fibromyalgia	49
Muscular Dystrophy	50
Tendonitis	50
Bursitis	51
Lupus	51
Back Pain (e.g., Herniated Disc)	52
Endocrine System Disorders	53
Diabetes Mellitus (Type 1 and Type 2)	53
Hyperthyroidism (e.g., Graves' Disease)	53

Hypothyroidism (e.g., Hashimoto's Thyroiditis)	54
Cushing's Syndrome	55
Addison's Disease	55
Polycystic Ovary Syndrome (PCOS)	56
Hyperparathyroidism	57
Pituitary Disorders (e.g., Pituitary Tumors)	57
Acromegaly	58
Osteoporosis	59
Renal and Urinary System Disorders	59
Integumentary System Disorders	66
Acne	66
Psoriasis	66
Eczema (Dermatitis)	67
Skin Cancer (e.g., Melanoma, Basal Cell Carcinoma)	68
Rosacea	68
Cellulitis	69
Herpes Zoster (Shingles)	69
Fungal Infections (e.g., Athlete's Foot)	70
Vitiligo	71
Urticaria (Hives)	71
Hematologic System Disorders	72
Anemia (e.g., Iron Deficiency Anemia)	72
Hemophilia	73
Leukemia	73
Lymphoma	74
Deep Vein Thrombosis (DVT)	75
Sickle Cell Disease	75
Thrombocytopenia	76
Hemochromatosis	77
Myelodysplastic Syndromes	77
Multiple Myeloma	78
Immune System Disorders	78
Rheumatoid Arthritis	79

Systemic Lupus Erythematosus (SLE)	79
Inflammatory Bowel Disease (IBD) - Crohn's & Ulcerative Colitis	80
Type 1 Diabetes Mellitus	81
Multiple Sclerosis	81
Psoriasis	82
Guillain-Barré Syndrome	83
Graves' Disease	83
Celiac Disease	84
Allergic Reactions (e.g., Hay Fever, Asthma, Anaphylaxis)	85
Oncological Disorders	85
Breast Cancer	85
Lung Cancer	86
Prostate Cancer	87
Colorectal Cancer	87
Leukemia	88
Lymphoma	89
Skin Cancer (Melanoma)	89
Pancreatic Cancer	90
Ovarian Cancer	91
Bladder Cancer	91
3 Adult Medical-Surgical Nursing Part 2	93
Perioperative Nursing Care	93
Chronic Disease Management	94
Pain Management in Medical-Surgical Patients	94
Nutritional Management in Medical-Surgical Conditions	95
Wound Care and Pressure Injury Management	96
Infectious Diseases and Isolation Precautions	96
Transfusion Reactions and Blood Product Administration	97
Intravenous Therapy and Central Venous Access	98
Emergency and Trauma Nursing	98
Shock: Types and Management	99
Sepsis and Septic Shock	99

Burns: Assessment and Management	100
Poisoning and Overdose Management	101
Bioterrorism and Disaster Response in Nursing	101
Palliative and End-of-Life Care in Medical-Surgical Settings	102
Patient Safety and Quality Improvement	103
Diagnostic Testing and Interpretation	103
4 Pharmacology	**105**
Pharmacokinetics and Pharmacodynamics	105
Medication Administration: Routes, Techniques, Safety	106
Drug Classifications and Indications	106
Analgesics and Pain Management Medications	107
Cardiovascular Medications: Antihypertensives, Diuretics, Anticoagulants	108
Respiratory Medications: Bronchodilators, Corticosteroids	108
Gastrointestinal Medications: Antacids, Laxatives, Antiemetics	109
Endocrine Medications: Insulins, Oral Hypoglycemics, Thyroid Medications	110
Renal and Urinary Medications: Diuretics, Antispasmodics	110
Neurological Medications: Anticonvulsants, Antiparkinsonians	111
Psychotropic Medications: Antidepressants, Antipsychotics, Anxiolytics	112
Anti-Infectives: Antibiotics, Antifungals, Antivirals	112
Oncology Medications: Chemotherapeutic Agents, Supportive Care Drugs	113
Immunosuppressants and Anti-Inflammatory Agents	114
Dermatological Medications: Topical Steroids, Antifungals	115
Ophthalmic and Otic Medications	115
Women's Health Medications: Hormonal Therapies, Contraceptives	116
Pediatric Medications: Dosing and Administration Considerations	117
Geriatric Medications: Polypharmacy and Drug Interactions	117
Emergency Medications: ACLS Drugs, Antidotes	118
Herbal Supplements and Alternative Therapies	119

Medication Calculations and Dosage Determinations	119
Adverse Drug Reactions and Side Effects	120
Medication Teaching and Compliance	121
5 Pediatric Nursing	122
Growth and Developmental Stages	122
Pediatric Assessment Techniques	123
Common Pediatric Medical Conditions	123
Pediatric Surgical Care	124
Pediatric Medication Administration	125
Pediatric Pain Assessment and Management	126
Immunizations and Preventive Care	126
Pediatric Nutrition and Feeding Issues	127
Genetic and Congenital Disorders	128
Pediatric Oncology Nursing	128
Pediatric Neurological Disorders	129
Pediatric Respiratory Disorders	130
Pediatric Cardiovascular Disorders	130
Pediatric Gastrointestinal Disorders	131
Pediatric Renal and Urinary Disorders	132
Pediatric Musculoskeletal Disorders	132
Pediatric Hematologic and Immunologic Disorders	133
Pediatric Endocrine Disorders	134
Child Abuse and Neglect: Identification and Reporting	134
Pediatric Mental Health Disorders	135
Pediatric Emergency Care	136
Care of the Hospitalized Child	136
Family Dynamics and Support in Pediatric Nursing	137
Pediatric Palliative and End-of-Life Care	138
6 Maternity and Women's Health Nursing	139
Prenatal Care and Assessments	139
Labor and Delivery Processes	140
Postpartum Nursing Care	140
Neonatal Nursing Care	141

High-Risk Pregnancies and Complications	142
Fetal Assessment and Monitoring	142
Breastfeeding and Newborn Nutrition	143
Common Gynecological Disorders	144
Women's Health: Preventive Care and Screenings	144
Contraception and Family Planning	145
Menopausal Care and Hormone Replacement Therapy	146
Maternal and Newborn Medications	146
Perinatal Loss and Grief Support	147
Women's Health Education and Counseling	148
7 Mental Health and Psychiatric Nursing	149
Mental Health Assessment and Diagnosis	149
Therapeutic Communication and Relationship Building	150
Anxiety and Mood Disorders	150
Schizophrenia and Other Psychotic Disorders	151
Personality and Impulse Control Disorders	152
Substance Use and Addictive Disorders	153
Eating Disorders	153
Child and Adolescent Mental Health Disorders	154
Elderly Mental Health Issues	155
Psychiatric Medications and Side Effects	156
Suicide Risk Assessment and Prevention	156
Crisis Intervention and Acute Psychiatric Care	157
Group and Family Therapy in Mental Health	158
Legal and Ethical Issues in Psychiatric Nursing	159
Community Mental Health Nursing	159
Mental Health Promotion and Education	160
8 Gerontological Nursing	162
Geriatric Assessment and Care Planning	162
Common Health Issues in Older Adults	163
Geriatric Syndromes: Falls, Incontinence, Delirium	164
Dementia and Alzheimer's Disease	164
Medication Management in Older Adults	165

		End-of-Life and Palliative Care in Geriatrics	166
		Long-Term Care and Rehabilitation	167
		Elder Abuse and Neglect	167
		Aging and Mental Health	168
		Chronic Disease Management in Older Adults	169
		Nutrition and Hydration in the Elderly	169
		Mobility and Safety Issues in Geriatrics	170
	9	Community and Public Health Nursing	172
		Epidemiology and Disease Surveillance	172
		Community Health Assessment and Planning	173
		Health Promotion and Disease Prevention Programs	174
		Global Health and Emerging Diseases	174
		Environmental and Occupational Health	175
		Disaster Preparedness and Response	176
		Health Education and Community Outreach	177
		School Health Nursing	177
		Home Health Nursing	178
		Public Health Policy and Advocacy	179
		Vulnerable Populations and Access to Care	179
		Cultural Competence and Health Literacy	180
	10	Leadership and Management in Nursing	182
		Nursing Leadership Styles and Theories	182
		Team Building and Interprofessional Collaboration	183
		Conflict Resolution and Negotiation	183
		Quality Improvement and Patient Safety	184
		Evidence-Based Practice and Research Utilization	185
		Healthcare Policy and Regulation	186
		Staff Development and Training	186
		Ethical Decision Making in Leadership	187
		Resource Management and Budgeting	188
		Health Informatics and Technology in Nursing	189
		Organizational Change and Innovation	189
	11	Comprehensive Test Preparation	191

NCLEX-RN Exam Structure and Format	191
Test-Taking Strategies and Tips	192
Prioritization and Delegation Questions	194
Select All That Apply (SATA) Question Strategies	195
Critical Thinking and Clinical Judgment	197
Time Management During the Exam	198
Stress Reduction and Anxiety Management	200
Review and Practice Questions	201
Continuing Education and Lifelong Learning	203
12 Claim Your Bonus Guide Here and Leave a Review:	205
BONUS: Complementary Study Guide Downloadable	205
Leave a Review!	206
Afterword	208
References	208
About the Author	210

Preface

FREE eBook When You Sign Up!

FREE When You Sign Up:
A Nurse's Quickstart Kit
Guide to Education, Career & Wellbeing
Mark Aquino BSN RN MHA
OasisNinja.com

BONUS When You Sign Up:
- Powerful newsletter
- More tips and tricks from fellow nurses
- Exclusive online community access

Scan this QR Code to Sign Up and Claim Your FREE eBook!

Or go to OasisNinja.com/free

FREE EBOOK: Sign Up for the FREE Nurse's Quickstart Kit!

Ready to unlock your full potential?

Go to OasisNinja.com/free to **fill out the form and grab your Quickstart Kit (it's FREE!)**

Or scan the QR Code above.

About the Author:

Mark Aquino RN

Mark Aquino is a registered nurse in California with a Bachelors of Science in Nursing and Masters of Health Administration from West Coast University. He has at worked in various psychiatric and mental health settings working alongside psychiatrists, therapists, and social workers and least 4 years of experience in the front lines as a visiting nurse in home health and hospice care. He is author of OASIS NINJA: A Home Health Nurse's Guide to Visits, Documentation, and Positive Patient Outcomes. This guide provides nurses with the information they need to provide quality care to their patients in the comfort of their own homes. He also writes books about how to live a good life and how to improve yourself on a daily basis. Learn more at OasisNinja.com.

—

Check out more books by this author at OasisNinja.com - https://oasisninja.com

"NCLEX RN Review Simplified: An NCLEX Review Study Guide Organized by Systems - Just the Essentials with Sample Questions"

Introduction: Embark on a simplified journey to NCLEX success with this innovative study guide. Tailored for aspiring nurses, this book demystifies complex topics, presenting a clear, concise, and comprehensive roadmap to mastering the NCLEX exam. Organized logically by body systems, it offers step-by-step guidance, ensuring a thorough understanding of each critical concept.

Chapter Overview:

1. **Fundamentals of Nursing Care:** Delve into the essentials of nursing, covering everything from basic care and comfort to infection control and safety guidelines. This foundational chapter sets the stage for a deeper understanding of nursing practice.
2. **Cardiovascular System Review:** Explore the anatomy, physiology, and common conditions of the cardiovascular system. Learn about relevant medications, nursing interventions, and patient education for cardiac patients.
3. **Respiratory System Mastery:** Gain insights into respiratory care, including assessment techniques, interventions for respiratory disorders, and key pharmacology concepts.
4. **Digestive System and Nutrition:** Understand the digestive process, common gastrointestinal disorders, and nutrition's role in patient care. This chapter covers dietary considerations, feeding techniques, and digestion-related pharmacology.
5. **Neurological System Insights:** Unpack the complexities of the nervous system, discussing neurological assessments, common neurological conditions, and appropriate nursing care strategies.
6. **Renal and Urinary Systems:** Dive into renal physiology, urinary disorders, and the nursing management of patients with urinary system

issues. Learn about dialysis, urinary catheterization, and related pharmacological treatments.
7. **Endocrine System Overview:** Examine endocrine disorders, hormonal therapies, and the nursing care of patients with endocrine imbalances.
8. **Musculoskeletal System:** Review musculoskeletal anatomy, common injuries and conditions, and nursing interventions for orthopedic patients.
9. **Reproductive and Maternal Health:** Focus on women's health, obstetrics, and neonatal care, including prenatal care, labor and delivery, and postpartum nursing considerations.
10. **Mental Health Nursing:** Navigate the realm of psychiatric nursing, discussing mental health disorders, therapeutic communication, and psychiatric medications.
11. **Oncology Nursing:** Understand the basics of cancer care, including common malignancies, chemotherapy, radiation therapy, and supportive care for oncology patients.
12. **Pediatric Nursing:** Learn about pediatric care from infancy through adolescence, covering growth and development, common pediatric conditions, and child-specific nursing interventions.
13. **Geriatric Nursing:** Explore the nuances of caring for the elderly, focusing on geriatric syndromes, age-related changes, and elder care strategies.
14. **Professional Issues and Ethics:** Discuss the legal and ethical aspects of nursing, including patient rights, informed consent, and professional conduct.
15. **NCLEX Exam Strategies:** Equip yourself with effective test-taking strategies, tips for tackling different question types, and ways to manage exam stress.

Know for each topic:

- Description
- Priority facts

- Nclex pearls
- Top safety tips
- Sample question with rationale

This book is an invaluable tool for any nursing student preparing for the NCLEX exam. It simplifies complex concepts, provides step-by-step guides, and organizes content in an easy-to-follow format, ensuring a clear path to success on the NCLEX.

——

Book Description

"NCLEX RN Review Simplified: An NCLEX Review Study Guide Organized by Systems - Just the Essentials with Sample Questions" is an essential guide for aspiring nurses aiming to master the NCLEX exam. This innovative study guide simplifies complex topics, presenting a clear, concise, and comprehensive roadmap to success. Organized logically by body systems, it offers step-by-step guidance, ensuring a thorough understanding of each critical concept.

From the fundamentals of nursing care, covering basic care, comfort, infection control, and safety guidelines, to detailed reviews of body systems such as cardiovascular, respiratory, digestive, and more, this book delves deep into each area. It provides insights into patient education for cardiac patients, respiratory care techniques, nutrition's role in patient care, neurological assessments, and nursing management of urinary disorders, among others. The guide also explores endocrine disorders, musculoskeletal anatomy, women's health, obstetrics, neonatal care, mental health, oncology, pediatric, and geriatric nursing, ensuring a holistic understanding of all nursing domains.

Additionally, the book addresses professional issues and ethics in nursing, emphasizing legal, ethical aspects, patient rights, and professional conduct. The final chapter equips readers with effective test-taking strategies, tips for handling different question types, and managing exam stress, culminating in a comprehensive conclusion that reinforces key points for NCLEX success.

Included are additional resources like practice questions, case studies, and a glossary of terms for further study and reinforcement. This guide is an invaluable tool for any nursing student preparing for the NCLEX exam, simplifying complex concepts, providing step-by-step guides, and organizing content in an easy-to-follow format to ensure a clear path to success on the NCLEX

- **System-Based Organization**: Content is logically organized by body systems, offering a structured and easy-to-follow learning path.
- **Fundamentals of Nursing Care**: A foundational chapter covering basic care, comfort, infection control, and safety guidelines sets the stage for advanced learning.
- **Comprehensive Body System Review**: In-depth exploration of the cardiovascular, respiratory, digestive, neurological, renal and urinary, and endocrine systems.
- **Specialized Nursing Areas**: Detailed chapters on musculoskeletal system, reproductive and maternal health, mental health, oncology, pediatric, and geriatric nursing.
- **Professional Issues and Ethics**: Insightful discussion on legal and ethical aspects of nursing, including patient rights, informed consent, and professional conduct.
- **Effective Test-Taking Strategies**: Equips you with strategies, tips for tackling different question types, and ways to manage exam stress.
- **Additional Learning Resources**: Includes practice questions, case studies, and a glossary of terms for further study and reinforcement.
- **Expertly Curated Content**: All topics are meticulously researched and presented in a manner that simplifies learning while ensuring comprehensive coverage.
- **Confidence-Building Approach**: The guide not only educates but also encourages readers to approach the NCLEX with confidence and competence.

"NCLEX RN Review Simplified" is more than just a study guide; it's a pathway to understanding and success, tailored for the modern nursing student preparing for the pivotal NCLEX exam.

FREE eBook When You Sign Up!

FREE When You Sign Up:
A Nurse's Quickstart Kit
Guide to Education, Career & Wellbeing
Mark Aquino BSN RN MHA
OASISNinja.com

<u>BONUS When You Sign Up:</u>
- *Powerful newsletter*
- *More tips and tricks from fellow nurses*
- *Exclusive online community access*

Scan this QR Code to Sign Up and Claim Your FREE eBook!

<u>Or go to OasisNinja.com/free</u>

FREE EBOOK: Sign Up for the FREE Nurse's Quickstart Kit!

Ready to unlock your full potential?

Go to OasisNinja.com/free to **fill out the form and grab your Quickstart Kit (it's FREE!)**

Or scan the QR Code above.

Acknowledgement

Acknowledgements: Thank you to my wife Diane for always supporting me. Thank you also to all my family, teachers, and home health agencies that acted as my counselors and consultants. And thank you to our baby girl Kristel Candace for being our bundle of joy.

1

Nursing Fundamentals

1. Basic Nursing Care and Comfort

- **Description:** This encompasses the fundamental aspects of nursing aimed at providing physical and emotional comfort to patients, including pain management, ensuring restful sleep, and addressing personal needs.
- **Priority Facts:** Knowledge of various pain assessment tools, understanding individualized comfort measures, and the importance of addressing psychological comfort alongside physical needs.
- **NCLEX Pearls:** Focus on patient-centered care, recognizing different types of pain, and the impact of comfort measures on patient recovery.
- **Top Safety Tips:** Regular pain assessments, appropriate administration and monitoring of analgesics, and ensuring the patient's environment promotes comfort.
- **Sample Question:** A nurse is caring for a patient who reports a pain level of 7 on a scale of 0 to 10. Which of the following actions should the nurse take FIRST?
- A. Administer prescribed pain medication.
- B. Reassess the patient's pain after 30 minutes.
- C. Adjust the patient's bedding and room temperature.
- D. Notify the healthcare provider.
- **Correct Answer:** A. Administer prescribed pain medication.

- **Rationale for Correct Answer:** Immediate pain relief is the priority for patients reporting high pain levels. Administering prescribed analgesics should be the first step.
- **Incorrect Answers:**
- B. Reassess the patient's pain after 30 minutes. (Rationale: While reassessment is important, it should be done after addressing the patient's immediate pain.)
- C. Adjust the patient's bedding and room temperature. (Rationale: Comfort measures are secondary to addressing severe pain.)
- D. Notify the healthcare provider. (Rationale: The provider should be notified if pain is uncontrolled or if there are changes in the patient's condition, but after initial pain management interventions.)

2. Patient Hygiene and Personal Care

- **Description:** Focuses on maintaining and assisting with patients' personal hygiene, which is vital for their physical and psychological well-being.
- **Priority Facts:** Techniques for safe and effective bed baths, oral care, perineal care, and maintaining skin integrity.
- **NCLEX Pearls:** Prioritize patient dignity and privacy, and tailor hygiene care to individual needs and conditions.
- **Top Safety Tips:** Use gentle techniques to avoid skin injury and respect patient preferences and limitations.
- **Sample Question:** What is the MOST important reason for performing frequent oral care on an unconscious patient?
- A. To prevent tooth decay.
- B. To keep the mouth moist and comfortable.
- C. To prevent pneumonia.
- D. To enhance the patient's appearance.
- **Correct Answer:** C. To prevent pneumonia.
- **Rationale:** For unconscious patients, frequent oral care is crucial to

prevent aspiration of oral bacteria, which can lead to pneumonia, a potentially life-threatening condition.
- **Incorrect Answers:**
- A. To prevent tooth decay. (Rationale: While oral hygiene is important for dental health, the immediate concern for unconscious patients is respiratory health.)
- B. To keep the mouth moist and comfortable. (Rationale: Comfort is important but not the primary concern in preventing serious complications.)
- D. To enhance the patient's appearance. (Rationale: Appearance is a lesser concern compared to preventing medical complications.)

3. Mobility and Positioning Techniques

- **Description:** Involves safe patient movement and positioning to promote physiological functioning and comfort, and prevent complications.
- **Priority Facts:** Proper body mechanics, understanding various positioning techniques, and use of mobility aids.
- **NCLEX Pearls:** Assess patient's mobility level before attempting movement and understand specific positioning requirements for different conditions.
- **Top Safety Tips:** Use assistive devices as needed, and frequently reposition immobile patients.
- **Sample Question:** When assisting a patient to walk from the bed to a chair, what is the BEST technique to prevent injury?
- A. Have another nurse assist you.
- B. Use a gait belt.
- C. Ask the patient to move quickly.
- D. Pull the patient's arms over your shoulders.
- **Correct Answer:** B. Use a gait belt.
- **Rationale:** A gait belt provides stability and support for the patient, reducing the risk of falls and enabling safer movement.

4. Infection Control Practices

- **Description:** Covers strategies to prevent and control infections, including hand hygiene, PPE use, and aseptic technique.
- **Priority Facts:** Standard and transmission-based precautions, proper techniques for handwashing, and PPE donning and doffing.
- **NCLEX Pearls:** Always adhere to infection control protocols and be aware of situations requiring specific precautions.
- **Top Safety Tips:** Strictly follow hand hygiene and PPE guidelines, and stay updated on infection control practices.
- **Sample Question:** Which action by the nurse demonstrates proper infection control when donning personal protective equipment (PPE)?
- A. Putting on gloves before gown.
- B. Tying the gown at the neck and waist.
- C. Wearing two pairs of gloves for extra protection.
- D. Wearing a mask instead of a respirator for tuberculosis.
- **Correct Answer:** B. Tying the gown at the neck and waist.
- **Rationale:** Properly securing the gown at the neck and waist ensures full coverage and protection, which is a key step in effective PPE use.

5. Safety Protocols and Patient Safety

- **Description:** Encompasses a range of practices aimed at ensuring the safety of patients in various healthcare settings.
- **Priority Facts:** Understanding fall risk assessment, medication safety checks, and emergency preparedness.
- **NCLEX Pearls:** Focus on identifying potential safety hazards and implementing appropriate preventive measures.
- **Top Safety Tips:** Conduct thorough safety assessments and adhere to protocols for medication administration and emergency response.
- **Sample Question:** When administering medication, what is the MOST important action for the nurse to ensure patient safety?
- A. Check the medication three times before administration.

- B. Administer the medication as quickly as possible.
- C. Only give medications prepared by another nurse.
- D. Leave the medications at the bedside if the patient is asleep.
- **Correct Answer:** A. Check the medication three times before administration.
- **Rationale:** Triple checking medication (before pulling from the drawer, when preparing it, and at the bedside) is crucial for preventing medication errors, ensuring the right patient receives the correct medication at the right dose, route, and time.

Environmental Safety and Emergency Preparedness

- **Description**: This area covers the strategies and protocols for ensuring safety in healthcare environments, particularly in the face of emergencies or disasters.
- **Priority Facts**: Familiarity with the hospital's emergency codes, understanding the use of safety equipment, and knowledge of evacuation procedures.
- **NCLEX Pearls**: Always be aware of the nearest exits and safety equipment in any healthcare setting. Regular participation in emergency drills is crucial.
- **Top Safety Tips**: Keep emergency pathways clear, regularly check emergency and safety equipment for functionality, and stay updated on the latest safety protocols.
- **Sample Question**: In case of a hospital fire, what is the nurse's FIRST priority? A. Evacuate patients immediately. B. Call the fire department. C. Close doors to contain the fire. D. Attempt to extinguish the fire.
- **Correct Answer**: C. Close doors to contain the fire. **Rationale**: The initial step in a fire situation is to contain it by closing doors, following the 'RACE' protocol (Rescue, Alarm, Contain, Extinguish).

Admission and Discharge Planning

- **Description**: This involves managing patient transitions into and out of healthcare facilities, ensuring continuity of care.
- **Priority Facts**: Accurate assessment of patient needs upon admission and thorough planning for post-discharge care.
- **NCLEX Pearls**: Involve the patient and their family in the planning process to ensure a smooth transition and comprehension of care plans.
- **Top Safety Tips**: Clarify medication instructions and follow-up care at discharge, and confirm understanding through teach-back methods.
- **Sample Question**: What is MOST important when planning a patient's discharge? A. Arranging transportation home. B. Ensuring the patient understands their medication regimen. C. Scheduling a follow-up appointment. D. Providing a list of local pharmacies.
- **Correct Answer**: B. Ensuring the patient understands their medication regimen. **Rationale**: Clear understanding of medication is critical to prevent complications and readmissions.

Patient Education Principles

- **Description**: Focuses on teaching patients about their health conditions and self-care practices.
- **Priority Facts**: Tailoring education to individual patient needs and learning styles, and verifying understanding.
- **NCLEX Pearls**: Utilize a variety of teaching methods and materials to cater to different learning preferences.
- **Top Safety Tips**: Always confirm patient understanding, especially regarding medications and self-care techniques.
- **Sample Question**: What is the BEST approach to teach a patient with limited literacy about a new medication? A. Provide detailed written instructions. B. Use medical jargon to explain the medication's effects. C. Demonstrate how to take the medication and have the patient repeat it. D. Ask the patient to read the medication label aloud.

- **Correct Answer**: C. Demonstrate how to take the medication and have the patient repeat it. **Rationale**: Demonstrations followed by patient return demonstrations are effective in ensuring understanding, particularly for patients with limited literacy.

Communication Skills in Nursing

- **Description**: Involves effectively exchanging information with patients, families, and healthcare teams.
- **Priority Facts**: Active listening, empathy, and clear, concise verbal and written communication.
- **NCLEX Pearls**: Always tailor communication to the patient's level of understanding and cultural background.
- **Top Safety Tips**: Verify understanding of all communications regarding patient care and treatment.
- **Sample Question**: What is the MOST effective way to communicate with a hearing-impaired patient? A. Speak loudly and slowly. B. Write down instructions. C. Use a professional sign language interpreter. D. Use complex medical terms to explain their condition.
- **Correct Answer**: C. Use a professional sign language interpreter. **Rationale**: Professional interpreters ensure accurate communication, respecting the patient's needs and promoting effective understanding.

Documentation and Charting

- **Description**: Involves accurately recording all aspects of patient care and treatment.
- **Priority Facts**: Timeliness, accuracy, and completeness of documentation are critical.
- **NCLEX Pearls**: Always document patient care and responses immediately after they occur.
- **Top Safety Tips**: Never document care before it is provided, and always ensure patient privacy when documenting.

- **Sample Question**: What should a nurse do if they make an error in charting? A. Erase the error and write over it. B. Leave the error and make a new entry. C. Use correction fluid to cover the error. D. Draw a single line through the error, initial, and date it.
- **Correct Answer**: D. Draw a single line through the error, initial, and date it. **Rationale**: This method maintains the integrity of the record while correcting the mistake transparently.

Delegation and Supervision in Nursing

- **Description**: Involves assigning tasks to appropriate healthcare team members and overseeing their performance.
- **Priority Facts**: Understand the scope of practice of different team members and match tasks to their qualifications.
- **NCLEX Pearls**: Ensure tasks are delegated to personnel with appropriate skills and verify understanding of the task.
- **Top Safety Tips**: Regularly monitor the performance of delegated tasks and provide feedback.
- **Sample Question**: Which task is MOST appropriate for a nurse to delegate to a nursing assistant?
- A. Initial patient assessment.
- B. Administering oral medications.
- C. Taking vital signs of a stable patient.
- D. Developing a nursing care plan.
- **Correct Answer**: C. Taking vital signs of a stable patient.
- **Rationale**: Vital sign measurement in a stable patient falls within the scope of practice of a nursing assistant and is a common task to delegate.

Ethical and Legal Considerations in Nursing

- **Description**: Focuses on adhering to moral principles and legal requirements in nursing practice.
- **Priority Facts**: Patient consent, confidentiality, and professional bound-

aries are key.
- **NCLEX Pearls**: Understand patient rights and nursing responsibilities to make ethical decisions.
- **Top Safety Tips**: Always obtain informed consent and maintain patient privacy.
- **Sample Question**: What should a nurse do if asked to perform a procedure that they believe is ethically wrong?
- A. Refuse to perform the procedure.
- B. Perform the procedure to avoid conflict.
- C. Discuss the concerns with a supervisor.
- D. Ignore personal beliefs and follow orders.
- **Correct Answer**: C. Discuss the concerns with a supervisor.
- **Rationale**: Nurses should address ethical concerns through proper channels, ensuring patient safety and professional integrity.

End-of-Life Care and Palliative Care

- **Description**: Involves providing compassionate care focused on comfort for patients with life-limiting illnesses.
- **Priority Facts**: Pain management, emotional support, and respecting patient and family wishes are essential.
- **NCLEX Pearls**: Communicate openly and honestly with patients and families about prognosis and care options.
- **Top Safety Tips**: Regularly assess and manage symptoms to maximize patient comfort.
- **Sample Question**: What is a nurse's priority when providing palliative care to a terminally ill patient?
- A. Cure the underlying disease.
- B. Provide aggressive life-sustaining treatments.
- C. Focus on relieving symptoms and providing comfort.
- D. Encourage the patient to make rapid decisions about care.
- **Correct Answer**: C. Focus on relieving symptoms and providing comfort.
- **Rationale**: Palliative care prioritizes comfort and quality of life for

terminally ill patients.

Advanced Directives and Living Wills

- **Description**: Legal documents stating a patient's preferences for medical care if they become unable to make decisions.
- **Priority Facts**: It's important to understand and respect these directives and ensure they are current and accessible.
- **NCLEX Pearls**: Regularly review and discuss advanced directives with patients and families.
- **Top Safety Tips**: Ensure that all healthcare team members are aware of and adhere to the directives.
- **Sample Question**: What is the nurse's role regarding a patient's living will?
- A. Disregard it if it conflicts with family wishes.
- B. Enforce the living will as legally binding.
- C. Modify the living will based on the patient's condition.
- D. Only consider it if the patient is terminally ill.
- **Correct Answer**: B. Enforce the living will as legally binding.
- **Rationale**: Nurses must respect and adhere to a patient's living will, as it reflects their choices for care.

Therapeutic Diets and Nutrition Support

- **Description**: Dietary modifications tailored to specific health conditions to improve patient outcomes.
- **Priority Facts**: Understanding different therapeutic diets and their indications is crucial (e.g., diabetic, renal).
- **NCLEX Pearls**: Assess patient dietary needs and preferences to ensure adherence to therapeutic diets.
- **Top Safety Tips**: Monitor patient response to the diet and adjust as necessary for optimal nutrition.
- **Sample Question**: What is a key consideration when managing a patient

on a low-sodium diet?
- A. Encouraging high fluid intake.
- B. Monitoring for signs of hypoglycemia.
- C. Avoiding foods high in potassium.
- D. Reading food labels for sodium content.
- **Correct Answer**: D. Reading food labels for sodium content.
- **Rationale**: For a low-sodium diet, it's important to be vigilant about hidden sodium in foods, which requires careful label reading.

Pain Assessment Tools

- **Description**: Tools and scales used to measure and evaluate pain intensity and characteristics in patients.
- **Priority Facts**: Common tools include the Numeric Rating Scale (NRS), Visual Analog Scale (VAS), and FLACC Scale for children.
- **NCLEX Pearls**: Choose the appropriate tool based on the patient's age, cognitive ability, and condition.
- **Top Safety Tips**: Regularly reassess pain using the same tool for consistency and accuracy.
- **Sample Question**: Which pain assessment tool is MOST appropriate for a non-verbal 3-year-old child?
- A. Numeric Rating Scale (NRS).
- B. Visual Analog Scale (VAS).
- C. FLACC (Face, Legs, Activity, Cry, Consolability) Scale.
- D. Simple Descriptive Pain Scale.
- **Correct Answer**: C. FLACC (Face, Legs, Activity, Cry, Consolability) Scale.
- **Rationale**: The FLACC Scale is designed for assessing pain in young children who cannot verbally communicate their pain intensity.

Non-Pharmacological Pain Management

- **Description**: Techniques to alleviate pain without the use of medications.
- **Priority Facts**: Includes methods like relaxation techniques, heat and cold therapy, massage, and acupuncture.
- **NCLEX Pearls**: These techniques can be used alone or in conjunction with pharmacological methods.
- **Top Safety Tips**: Assess the patient's response to these techniques and adjust as needed.
- **Sample Question**: Which non-pharmacological intervention is BEST for a patient experiencing low back pain?
- A. Applying a cold pack to the area.
- B. Administering an opioid analgesic.
- C. Encouraging increased fluid intake.
- D. Performing deep-breathing exercises.
- **Correct Answer**: A. Applying a cold pack to the area.
- **Rationale**: Cold therapy can help reduce inflammation and alleviate pain in conditions like low back pain.

Therapeutic Communication Techniques

- **Description**: Skills used in nursing to enhance communication with patients and improve their care experience.
- **Priority Facts**: Includes active listening, empathy, open-ended questions, and reflection.
- **NCLEX Pearls**: Effective therapeutic communication can significantly improve patient outcomes and satisfaction.
- **Top Safety Tips**: Always ensure patient understanding and provide a supportive environment for open communication.
- **Sample Question**: Which is an example of using therapeutic communication with a patient?
- A. Offering advice based on personal experiences.
- B. Using medical jargon to explain a diagnosis.

- C. Asking the patient how they feel about their diagnosis.
- D. Telling the patient what they should do.
- **Correct Answer**: C. Asking the patient how they feel about their diagnosis.
- **Rationale**: Asking open-ended questions like how a patient feels encourages expression and helps in understanding their perspective.

Cultural Competency in Nursing Care

- **Description**: The ability to provide care that respects the beliefs, values, and practices of different cultures.
- **Priority Facts**: Involves understanding cultural influences on health behaviors and preferences.
- **NCLEX Pearls**: Respect for cultural differences is key in providing patient-centered care.
- **Top Safety Tips**: Be aware of cultural beliefs that might affect health decisions and communication.
- **Sample Question**: What is an essential aspect of cultural competency in nursing care?
- A. Assuming all patients from a certain culture have the same beliefs.
- B. Avoiding discussions about the patient's cultural background.
- C. Adapting care to meet the cultural needs of the patient.
- D. Using one's own cultural values as a guide for patient care.
- **Correct Answer**: C. Adapting care to meet the cultural needs of the patient.
- **Rationale**: Cultural competency involves tailoring care to respect and meet the unique cultural needs of each patient.

Health Disparities and Social Determinants of Health

- **Description**: The study of how social, economic, and environmental factors contribute to health inequalities.
- **Priority Facts**: Includes factors like socioeconomic status, education, neighborhood, and physical environment.
- **NCLEX Pearls**: Nurses play a crucial role in identifying and addressing

health disparities.
- **Top Safety Tips**: Advocate for equitable healthcare access and address social determinants in care planning.
- **Sample Question**: Which factor is considered a social determinant of health?
- A. Genetic predisposition to diabetes.
- B. Access to healthcare services.
- C. Blood type.
- D. Personal choices regarding diet and exercise.
- **Correct Answer**: B. Access to healthcare services.
- **Rationale**: Social determinants of health, like access to healthcare services, significantly influence individual and community health outcomes.

Health Promotion and Disease Prevention

- **Description**: Involves strategies to help patients maintain or enhance their health and prevent diseases.
- **Priority Facts**: Understanding risk factors, screening guidelines, and lifestyle modifications.
- **NCLEX Pearls**: Focus on patient education regarding healthy behaviors and routine screenings.
- **Top Safety Tips**: Tailor health promotion strategies to each patient's individual needs and risk factors.
- **Sample Question**: What is a primary focus of health promotion for a patient with a family history of hypertension?
- A. Regular blood pressure monitoring.
- B. Prescribing antihypertensive medications preemptively.
- C. Advising the patient to avoid all dietary sodium.
- D. Encouraging biannual physical examinations.
- **Correct Answer**: A. Regular blood pressure monitoring.
- **Rationale**: Regular monitoring is key in early detection and management of hypertension, especially with a family history.

Nursing Process: Assessment, Diagnosis, Planning, Implementation, Evaluation

- **Description**: A systematic approach to patient care involving five critical steps.
- **Priority Facts**: Each step is distinct but interrelated, forming a continuous cycle of patient care.
- **NCLEX Pearls**: Always start with a thorough assessment before moving to diagnosis and planning.
- **Top Safety Tips**: Continually evaluate and adjust care plans based on patient response.
- **Sample Question**: What is the FIRST step a nurse should take when caring for a patient with chest pain?
- A. Administer pain medication.
- B. Perform a thorough assessment.
- C. Prepare the patient for surgery.
- D. Educate the patient about heart health.
- **Correct Answer**: B. Perform a thorough assessment.
- **Rationale**: Assessment is the first step in the nursing process and is crucial for determining the appropriate course of action.

Vital Signs Monitoring

- **Description**: Regular checking of body temperature, pulse, respiration, and blood pressure.
- **Priority Facts**: Vital signs offer critical information about the body's physiological state.
- **NCLEX Pearls**: Accurate measurement and interpretation of vital signs are essential in patient assessment.
- **Top Safety Tips**: Ensure the equipment is calibrated and appropriate for the patient (e.g., cuff size for blood pressure).
- **Sample Question**: When measuring blood pressure, what is essential to ensure accuracy?

- A. Using a cuff of the correct size.
- B. Taking the measurement after physical activity.
- C. Measuring only on the left arm.
- D. Having the patient stand during measurement.
- **Correct Answer**: A. Using a cuff of the correct size.
- **Rationale**: An incorrectly sized cuff can lead to inaccurate blood pressure readings.

Fluid and Electrolyte Balance

- **Description**: Maintaining the right balance of fluids and electrolytes in the body, crucial for physiological processes.
- **Priority Facts**: Imbalances can lead to conditions like dehydration, overhydration, hyponatremia, or hyperkalemia.
- **NCLEX Pearls**: Monitor intake and output, and be alert for signs of imbalance (e.g., edema, confusion).
- **Top Safety Tips**: Administer IV fluids and electrolyte replacements according to physician orders and patient needs.
- **Sample Question**: What is a common sign of hypokalemia (low potassium)?
- A. Muscle weakness.
- B. Edema.
- C. Hypertension.
- D. Bradycardia.
- **Correct Answer**: A. Muscle weakness.
- **Rationale**: Hypokalemia often presents with muscle weakness and can progress to more severe symptoms.

Acid-Base Balance

- **Description**: The maintenance of the correct pH level in the body's fluids.
- **Priority Facts**: Imbalances can be either metabolic (e.g., ketoacidosis) or respiratory (e.g., hypoventilation).

- **NCLEX Pearls**: Use arterial blood gas (ABG) results to assess acid-base balance.
- **Top Safety Tips**: Monitor patients with conditions that can affect acid-base balance closely (e.g., diabetes, respiratory disorders).
- **Sample Question**: What is the initial action for a nurse when an ABG shows a pH of 7.32?
- A. Administer sodium bicarbonate.
- B. Increase the patient's oxygen flow rate.
- C. Assess the patient for symptoms of acidosis.
- D. Immediately start CPR.
- **Correct Answer**: C. Assess the patient for symptoms of acidosis.
- **Rationale**: A pH of 7.32 indicates acidosis; assessment for symptoms is crucial to determine the underlying cause and appropriate intervention.

Aseptic Technique and Sterile Procedures

- **Description**: Methods used to prevent contamination by pathogens and maintain sterility during medical procedures.
- **Priority Facts**: Key components include hand hygiene, use of personal protective equipment (PPE), and proper sterilization of equipment.
- **NCLEX Pearls**: Always follow standard precautions and specific sterile techniques for invasive procedures.
- **Top Safety Tips**: Regularly check integrity of sterile packages, avoid touching sterile surfaces with non-sterile items.
- **Sample Question**: What is the MOST important action to maintain sterility when performing a sterile procedure?
- A. Wearing gloves at all times.
- B. Keeping sterile items above waist level.
- C. Disinfecting the work surface beforehand.
- D. Having another nurse observe the procedure.
- **Correct Answer**: B. Keeping sterile items above waist level.

- **Rationale**: Keeping sterile items above waist level is crucial to avoid contamination from non-sterile surfaces.

Oxygenation and Ventilation

- **Description**: Processes involved in ensuring adequate oxygen is delivered to the body's tissues and carbon dioxide is removed.
- **Priority Facts**: Monitoring oxygen saturation, understanding the use of oxygen delivery systems (like nasal cannula, masks).
- **NCLEX Pearls**: Be aware of signs of hypoxia (like cyanosis, confusion) and the appropriate interventions.
- **Top Safety Tips**: Regularly check the oxygen flow rate and ensure the patient's comfort with the oxygen delivery device.
- **Sample Question**: When caring for a patient with COPD who requires supplemental oxygen, what is the MOST important safety consideration?
- A. Administering high-flow oxygen continuously.
- B. Monitoring for signs of oxygen toxicity.
- C. Using the lowest effective oxygen concentration.
- D. Encouraging deep breathing exercises every hour.
- **Correct Answer**: C. Using the lowest effective oxygen concentration.
- **Rationale**: For patients with COPD, it's essential to use the lowest effective oxygen concentration to avoid suppressing their respiratory drive.

Basic Life Support (BLS) and Cardiopulmonary Resuscitation (CPR)

- **Description**: Emergency procedures used to maintain circulation and breathing in a person who is in cardiac arrest.
- **Priority Facts**: BLS steps include checking responsiveness, calling for help, providing chest compressions, and rescue breathing.
- **NCLEX Pearls**: Remember the CPR ratio of 30 compressions to 2 breaths for adults.
- **Top Safety Tips**: Ensure correct hand placement and adequate depth and

rate of compressions.
- **Sample Question**: What is the FIRST action a nurse should take when encountering an unresponsive adult patient?
- A. Begin chest compressions immediately.
- B. Check the patient's airway and breathing.
- C. Call for help and get an AED (Automated External Defibrillator) if available.
- D. Provide two rescue breaths.
- **Correct Answer**: C. Call for help and get an AED (Automated External Defibrillator) if available.
- **Rationale**: The first step in BLS for an unresponsive adult is to call for help and get an AED, as early defibrillation is critical in the survival of cardiac arrest.

2

Adult Medical-Surgical Nursing Part 1

Cardiovascular System Disorders

Coronary Artery Disease (CAD)

- **Description**: A condition characterized by reduced blood flow to the heart muscle due to plaque buildup in the coronary arteries.
- **Priority Facts**: Risk factors include high cholesterol, smoking, hypertension, and diabetes.
- **NCLEX Pearls**: Focus on patient education about lifestyle modifications and adherence to medication regimens.
- **Top Safety Tips**: Monitor patients for signs of chest pain, and ensure rapid response to potential angina or heart attack symptoms.
- **Sample Question**: What is a key nursing intervention for a patient with stable CAD?
- A. Administer nitroglycerin for chest pain.
- B. Prepare for immediate coronary bypass surgery.
- C. Encourage high-intensity exercise.
- D. Limit fluid intake to reduce blood volume.

- **Correct Answer**: A. Administer nitroglycerin for chest pain.
- **Rationale**: Nitroglycerin is used to relieve chest pain in CAD by dilating coronary arteries and improving blood flow to the heart muscle.

Hypertension (High Blood Pressure)

- **Description**: A chronic condition where the blood pressure in the arteries is consistently elevated.
- **Priority Facts**: Primary hypertension has no identifiable cause, while secondary hypertension results from an underlying condition.
- **NCLEX Pearls**: Regular monitoring of blood pressure and adherence to prescribed medications are crucial.
- **Top Safety Tips**: Educate patients about lifestyle changes, such as diet and exercise, to manage blood pressure.
- **Sample Question**: Which lifestyle modification is MOST effective in controlling high blood pressure?
- A. Increasing protein intake.
- B. Reducing dietary sodium.
- C. Taking aspirin daily.
- D. Drinking two liters of water per day.
- **Correct Answer**: B. Reducing dietary sodium.
- **Rationale**: Reducing sodium intake is a key factor in lowering blood pressure, as it helps to reduce fluid retention.

Heart Failure

- **Description**: A chronic condition in which the heart is unable to pump sufficiently to maintain blood flow to meet the body's needs.
- **Priority Facts**: Common symptoms include shortness of breath, fatigue, and fluid retention.
- **NCLEX Pearls**: Monitoring fluid status, daily weight, and adherence to a low-sodium diet are essential.
- **Top Safety Tips**: Assess for signs of fluid overload and educate patients

on recognizing worsening symptoms.
- **Sample Question**: What is the primary goal of treatment for a patient with heart failure?
- A. Cure the underlying heart disease.
- B. Increase heart rate to improve cardiac output.
- C. Reduce fluid volume overload.
- D. Maintain a high-sodium diet.
- **Correct Answer**: C. Reduce fluid volume overload.
- **Rationale**: Managing fluid volume is crucial in heart failure to reduce symptoms and prevent exacerbation of the condition.

Arrhythmias (e.g., Atrial Fibrillation)

- **Description**: Disorders of heart rhythm, ranging from harmless to life-threatening.
- **Priority Facts**: Atrial fibrillation is a common type, characterized by irregular and often rapid heart rate.
- **NCLEX Pearls**: Understanding the type of arrhythmia is key to managing it correctly.
- **Top Safety Tips**: Monitor cardiac rhythm and be aware of symptoms like palpitations or dizziness.
- **Sample Question**: What is a priority nursing action for a patient newly diagnosed with atrial fibrillation?
- A. Prepare for immediate defibrillation.
- B. Start an IV line for fluid replacement.
- C. Monitor for signs of stroke.
- D. Encourage aerobic exercise to strengthen the heart.
- **Correct Answer**: C. Monitor for signs of stroke.
- **Rationale**: Patients with atrial fibrillation are at an increased risk for stroke due to the potential for forming blood clots in the heart.

Cardiomyopathies

- **Description**: A group of diseases that affect the heart muscle, often leading to heart failure.
- **Priority Facts**: Types include dilated, hypertrophic, and restrictive cardiomyopathy.
- **NCLEX Pearls**: Focus on management of symptoms and prevention of complications.
- **Top Safety Tips**: Monitor for signs of heart failure and educate patients on medication adherence and lifestyle changes.
- **Sample Question**: What is an important aspect of care for a patient with hypertrophic cardiomyopathy?
- A. Encouraging weight lifting to strengthen the heart.
- B. Administering high-dose diuretics regularly.
- C. Monitoring for arrhythmias and obstruction to blood flow.
- D. Promoting a high-salt diet to increase blood volume.
- **Correct Answer**: C. Monitoring for arrhythmias and obstruction to blood flow.
- **Rationale**: Hypertrophic cardiomyopathy can lead to arrhythmias and obstructive symptoms, which need to be closely monitored for effective management.

Peripheral Artery Disease (PAD)

- **Description**: A common circulatory problem where narrowed arteries reduce blood flow to the limbs.
- **Priority Facts**: Risk factors include smoking, diabetes, obesity, and high blood pressure.
- **NCLEX Pearls**: Educate patients on lifestyle changes and the importance of foot care.
- **Top Safety Tips**: Monitor for signs of decreased perfusion to the limbs, like pain, changes in skin color, or temperature.
- **Sample Question**: What is an important nursing intervention for a

patient with PAD?
- A. Encouraging dependent positioning of the legs.
- B. Promoting smoking cessation.
- C. Applying a heating pad to the affected area.
- D. Restricting fluid intake.
- **Correct Answer**: B. Promoting smoking cessation.
- **Rationale**: Smoking cessation is crucial in PAD management as smoking contributes to arterial narrowing and decreased blood flow.

Valvular Heart Diseases (e.g., Mitral Valve Prolapse)

- **Description**: Disorders involving the heart valves, such as mitral valve prolapse, leading to improper blood flow within the heart.
- **Priority Facts**: Symptoms can include palpitations, shortness of breath, and fatigue.
- **NCLEX Pearls**: Regular monitoring for changes in symptoms and heart sounds is essential.
- **Top Safety Tips**: Educate patients about endocarditis prophylaxis if needed and the importance of regular follow-up.
- **Sample Question**: What symptom may indicate worsening mitral valve prolapse?
- A. Increased appetite.
- B. Sudden weight gain.
- C. Decreased urinary output.
- D. Shortness of breath.
- **Correct Answer**: D. Shortness of breath.
- **Rationale**: Shortness of breath may indicate that the valve dysfunction is worsening, leading to heart failure symptoms.

Congenital Heart Diseases

- **Description**: Heart abnormalities present at birth, affecting the heart's structure and function.
- **Priority Facts**: Common types include septal defects, valve malformations, and Tetralogy of Fallot.
- **NCLEX Pearls**: Monitoring for growth delays, feeding difficulties, and cyanosis in infants.
- **Top Safety Tips**: Educate families about signs of heart failure and the importance of immunizations and regular check-ups.
- **Sample Question**: What is a key consideration in the care of an infant with congenital heart disease?
- A. Encouraging unrestricted physical activity.
- B. Monitoring for signs of heart failure.
- C. Limiting oral fluid intake.
- D. Administering high-dose aspirin therapy.
- **Correct Answer**: B. Monitoring for signs of heart failure.
- **Rationale**: Infants with congenital heart disease are at risk for heart failure, and it is essential to monitor for related signs and symptoms.

Deep Vein Thrombosis (DVT) and Pulmonary Embolism

- **Description**: DVT is the formation of a blood clot in a deep vein, typically in the legs, which can lead to a pulmonary embolism if dislodged.
- **Priority Facts**: Risk factors include prolonged immobility, surgery, and certain medical conditions.
- **NCLEX Pearls**: Prophylactic measures include leg exercises, early ambulation, and anticoagulant therapy.
- **Top Safety Tips**: Assess for signs of DVT, such as leg pain, swelling, and redness; monitor for respiratory distress.
- **Sample Question**: What is a priority nursing action for preventing DVT in postoperative patients?
- A. Keeping the patient on strict bed rest.

- B. Administering prophylactic anticoagulants as ordered.
- C. Applying heat to the lower extremities.
- D. Massaging the patient's legs daily.
- **Correct Answer**: B. Administering prophylactic anticoagulants as ordered.
- **Rationale**: Prophylactic anticoagulants are key in preventing DVT, especially in patients with risk factors like recent surgery.

Aortic Aneurysms

- **Description**: An abnormal enlargement or bulging of the aorta, the main artery of the body.
- **Priority Facts**: Risk factors include hypertension, smoking, and atherosclerosis.
- **NCLEX Pearls**: Be alert for signs of rupture, such as severe back or abdominal pain.
- **Top Safety Tips**: Regular monitoring of blood pressure and size of the aneurysm.
- **Sample Question**: What is a critical sign of a ruptured aortic aneurysm that requires immediate attention?
- A. Gradual onset of shortness of breath.
- B. Intense, sudden back pain.
- C. Slow, steady heartbeat.
- D. Mild abdominal discomfort.
- **Correct Answer**: B. Intense, sudden back pain.
- **Rationale**: Sudden, intense back or abdominal pain can indicate a ruptured aortic aneurysm, a life-threatening emergency.

Respiratory System Disorders

Asthma

- **Description**: A chronic respiratory condition characterized by airway inflammation and hyperreactivity leading to wheezing, shortness of breath, chest tightness, and coughing.
- **Priority Facts**: Triggers include allergens, exercise, cold air, and stress.
- **NCLEX Pearls**: Focus on patient education about trigger avoidance and proper inhaler technique.
- **Top Safety Tips**: Monitor peak flow readings and recognize early signs of exacerbations.
- **Sample Question**: What is the MOST important action for a nurse when caring for a patient experiencing an acute asthma attack?
- A. Encourage deep breathing and relaxation techniques.
- B. Administer a short-acting bronchodilator via nebulizer or inhaler.
- C. Initiate high-flow oxygen therapy immediately.
- D. Perform chest physiotherapy to loosen secretions.
- **Correct Answer**: B. Administer a short-acting bronchodilator via nebulizer or inhaler.
- **Rationale**: Quick-relief bronchodilators are the first line of treatment during an acute asthma attack to relieve bronchospasm.

Chronic Obstructive Pulmonary Disease (COPD)

- **Description**: A group of lung diseases, including emphysema and chronic bronchitis, that block airflow and make breathing difficult.
- **Priority Facts**: Major cause is long-term exposure to lung irritants, especially cigarette smoke.
- **NCLEX Pearls**: Emphasize smoking cessation and pulmonary rehabilitation.
- **Top Safety Tips**: Monitor oxygen saturation and avoid high oxygen concentrations to prevent CO2 retention.

- **Sample Question**: What is a priority nursing intervention for a patient with COPD?
- A. Encourage bed rest to conserve energy.
- B. Administer oxygen at high flow rates.
- C. Provide bronchodilators and encourage pursed-lip breathing.
- D. Limit fluids to decrease mucus production.
- **Correct Answer**: C. Provide bronchodilators and encourage pursed-lip breathing.
- **Rationale**: Bronchodilators improve airflow, and pursed-lip breathing helps with better expiration and prevents air trapping.

Pneumonia

- **Description**: An infection that inflames the air sacs in one or both lungs, which may fill with fluid or pus.
- **Priority Facts**: Can be caused by bacteria, viruses, or fungi; community-acquired and hospital-acquired pneumonia are major types.
- **NCLEX Pearls**: Focus on early detection, antibiotic therapy, and supportive care.
- **Top Safety Tips**: Monitor respiratory status and oxygenation, and encourage coughing and deep breathing exercises.
- **Sample Question**: Which intervention is MOST important for a patient diagnosed with pneumonia?
- A. Maintaining bed rest in a high Fowler's position.
- B. Administering prescribed antibiotics promptly.
- C. Providing antipyretics only when fever exceeds 101°F.
- D. Restricting fluid intake to prevent fluid overload.
- **Correct Answer**: B. Administering prescribed antibiotics promptly.
- **Rationale**: Timely administration of antibiotics is crucial in treating bacterial pneumonia and preventing complications.

ADULT MEDICAL-SURGICAL NURSING PART 1

Pulmonary Embolism

- **Description**: A blockage in one of the pulmonary arteries in the lungs, typically caused by blood clots that travel from the legs or other parts of the body.
- **Priority Facts**: Risk factors include deep vein thrombosis, prolonged immobility, and certain medical conditions.
- **NCLEX Pearls**: Be alert for symptoms like sudden shortness of breath, chest pain, and rapid heart rate.
- **Top Safety Tips**: Monitor for signs of DVT, provide anticoagulant therapy as prescribed, and educate about prevention.
- **Sample Question**: What is the FIRST nursing action if a pulmonary embolism is suspected?
- A. Start CPR.
- B. Administer a bolus of IV fluids.
- C. Place the patient in Trendelenburg position.
- D. Administer supplemental oxygen and notify the physician.
- **Correct Answer**: D. Administer supplemental oxygen and notify the physician.
- **Rationale**: Providing oxygen can help alleviate hypoxemia, and immediate medical evaluation is necessary for diagnosis and treatment.

Tuberculosis

- **Description**: A potentially serious infectious bacterial disease that mainly affects the lungs.
- **Priority Facts**: Caused by Mycobacterium tuberculosis, it is spread through airborne particles from coughs or sneezes.
- **NCLEX Pearls**: Focus on adherence to long-term antibiotic therapy and infection control measures.
- **Top Safety Tips**: Use airborne precautions for patients suspected or diagnosed with active TB.
- **Sample Question**: What is essential in the care of a patient with active

tuberculosis?
- A. Placing the patient in a room with negative air pressure.
- B. Administering a single antibiotic for treatment.
- C. Encouraging high-intensity exercise to improve lung function.
- D. Isolating the patient only when coughing or sneezing.
- **Correct Answer**: A. Placing the patient in a room with negative air pressure.
- **Rationale**: Negative air pressure rooms are used to prevent the spread of airborne particles and protect others from infection.

Lung Cancer

- **Description**: A type of cancer that begins in the lungs, often associated with smoking, though it can also occur in non-smokers.
- **Priority Facts**: Symptoms include a persistent cough, chest pain, and shortness of breath.
- **NCLEX Pearls**: Emphasize smoking cessation and early detection through screening in at-risk populations.
- **Top Safety Tips**: Monitor respiratory status and manage symptoms like pain and dyspnea.
- **Sample Question**: What is a key component of nursing care for a patient undergoing treatment for lung cancer?
- A. Limiting physical activity to reduce fatigue.
- B. Providing high-flow oxygen continuously.
- C. Monitoring for signs of infection and respiratory distress.
- D. Encouraging a high-carbohydrate diet.
- **Correct Answer**: C. Monitoring for signs of infection and respiratory distress.
- **Rationale**: Patients with lung cancer are at increased risk for respiratory complications and infections, especially during treatment.

Pulmonary Hypertension

- **Description**: A type of high blood pressure that affects the arteries in the lungs and the right side of the heart.
- **Priority Facts**: Can lead to shortness of breath, dizziness, and chest pain.
- **NCLEX Pearls**: Focus on managing underlying causes and symptoms.
- **Top Safety Tips**: Monitor for worsening respiratory status and adhere to prescribed treatment regimens.
- **Sample Question**: What is an important nursing consideration for a patient with pulmonary hypertension?
- A. Encouraging regular, strenuous exercise.
- B. Administering sedatives frequently for comfort.
- C. Monitoring for signs of right-sided heart failure.
- D. Restricting all fluid intake.
- **Correct Answer**: C. Monitoring for signs of right-sided heart failure.
- **Rationale**: Pulmonary hypertension can strain the right side of the heart, leading to heart failure, necessitating close monitoring of cardiac function.

Cystic Fibrosis

- **Description**: A genetic disorder affecting the lungs and digestive system, characterized by thick, sticky mucus that can clog the lungs and obstruct the pancreas.
- **Priority Facts**: Symptoms include persistent cough, frequent lung infections, and poor weight gain.
- **NCLEX Pearls**: Management includes chest physiotherapy, nutritional support, and medications to thin mucus.
- **Top Safety Tips**: Monitor lung function and nutritional status, and educate on infection prevention.
- **Sample Question**: What is a primary nursing intervention for a patient with cystic fibrosis?
- A. Limit physical activity to conserve energy.

- B. Perform chest physiotherapy to aid in mucus clearance.
- C. Administer high-dose corticosteroids regularly.
- D. Encourage a low-fat diet.
- **Correct Answer**: B. Perform chest physiotherapy to aid in mucus clearance.
- **Rationale**: Chest physiotherapy is vital in cystic fibrosis care to help clear mucus from the lungs and improve breathing.

Pleural Effusion

- **Description**: A buildup of fluid between the layers of tissue that line the lungs and chest cavity.
- **Priority Facts**: Can result from various conditions, including pneumonia, heart failure, and cancer.
- **NCLEX Pearls**: Focus on identifying the underlying cause and managing symptoms.
- **Top Safety Tips**: Monitor for respiratory distress and chest pain, and ensure appropriate treatment is administered.
- **Sample Question**: What is the MOST appropriate initial nursing action for a patient suspected of having a pleural effusion?
- A. Position the patient flat on their back.
- B. Administer high-dose diuretics.
- C. Prepare the patient for a chest x-ray.
- D. Start chest compressions.
- **Correct Answer**: C. Prepare the patient for a chest x-ray.
- **Rationale**: A chest x-ray is essential for confirming the diagnosis of pleural effusion and determining its cause and extent.

Sleep Apnea

- **Description**: A sleep disorder characterized by repeated stopping and starting of breathing during sleep.
- **Priority Facts**: Risk factors include obesity, narrow airway, smoking,

and use of alcohol or sedatives.
- **NCLEX Pearls**: Emphasize the importance of continuous positive airway pressure (CPAP) therapy and lifestyle modifications.
- **Top Safety Tips**: Educate about the risks of untreated sleep apnea, including cardiovascular problems.
- **Sample Question**: What is a key nursing action for a patient with obstructive sleep apnea?
- A. Encouraging the use of sleep sedatives before bedtime.
- B. Advising to sleep on the back for better airway patency.
- C. Educating about the proper use of CPAP.
- D. Restricting all fluid intake at night.
- **Correct Answer**: C. Educating about the proper use of CPAP.
- **Rationale**: CPAP is the primary treatment for obstructive sleep apnea, helping to keep the airway open during sleep.

Gastrointestinal System Disorders

Gastroesophageal Reflux Disease (GERD)

- **Description**: A digestive disorder where stomach acid frequently flows back into the esophagus, causing irritation.
- **Priority Facts**: Common triggers include fatty foods, caffeine, alcohol, and smoking.
- **NCLEX Pearls**: Lifestyle modifications are key in managing GERD symptoms.
- **Top Safety Tips**: Educate patients about avoiding trigger foods and the importance of medication adherence.
- **Sample Question**: What lifestyle change is MOST effective for managing symptoms in a patient with GERD?
- A. Eating large meals right before bedtime.
- B. Elevating the head of the bed during sleep.
- C. Increasing intake of caffeinated beverages.
- D. Engaging in high-intensity exercise immediately after meals.

- **Correct Answer**: B. Elevating the head of the bed during sleep.
- **Rationale**: Elevating the head of the bed helps prevent acid reflux during sleep, reducing GERD symptoms.

Peptic Ulcers

- **Description**: Sores that develop on the lining of the stomach, lower esophagus, or small intestine, often caused by H. pylori bacteria or long-term use of NSAIDs.
- **Priority Facts**: Symptoms include burning stomach pain, bloating, and heartburn.
- **NCLEX Pearls**: Treatment includes antibiotics for H. pylori and medications to reduce stomach acid.
- **Top Safety Tips**: Monitor for signs of complications, such as gastrointestinal bleeding.
- **Sample Question**: What is a priority nursing intervention for a patient with a peptic ulcer?
- A. Encouraging the intake of spicy foods to stimulate healing.
- B. Administering prescribed medications and monitoring for side effects.
- C. Instructing the patient to fast for prolonged periods.
- D. Recommending the regular use of NSAIDs for pain management.
- **Correct Answer**: B. Administering prescribed medications and monitoring for side effects.
- **Rationale**: Medications are crucial in treating peptic ulcers, and monitoring for side effects ensures patient safety.

Crohn's Disease

- **Description**: A type of inflammatory bowel disease (IBD) that can affect any part of the gastrointestinal tract, causing inflammation, pain, and digestive issues.
- **Priority Facts**: Symptoms include abdominal pain, severe diarrhea, fatigue, and weight loss.

- **NCLEX Pearls**: Management focuses on reducing inflammation and maintaining nutritional status.
- **Top Safety Tips**: Monitor for signs of bowel obstruction and nutritional deficiencies.
- **Sample Question**: What dietary modification is typically recommended for a patient with Crohn's disease?
- A. High-fiber diet.
- B. Lactose-rich diet.
- C. Low-residue diet.
- D. Unlimited fluid intake.
- **Correct Answer**: C. Low-residue diet.
- **Rationale**: A low-residue diet reduces the amount of undigested food passing through the intestines, decreasing bowel irritation.

Ulcerative Colitis

- **Description**: A chronic inflammatory bowel disease affecting the colon and rectum, characterized by inflammation and ulcers in the lining of the large intestine.
- **Priority Facts**: Common symptoms include bloody diarrhea, abdominal pain, and urgency to defecate.
- **NCLEX Pearls**: Long-term management may include medication, dietary changes, and sometimes surgery.
- **Top Safety Tips**: Monitor for signs of dehydration and electrolyte imbalances due to diarrhea.
- **Sample Question**: What is an important nursing action for managing a patient with ulcerative colitis during a flare-up?
- A. Encouraging vigorous abdominal exercises.
- B. Administering anti-diarrheal medications as prescribed.
- C. Suggesting a high-fat diet to increase caloric intake.
- D. Restricting all oral intake until symptoms subside.
- **Correct Answer**: B. Administering anti-diarrheal medications as prescribed.

- **Rationale**: Anti-diarrheal medications can help reduce the severity of diarrhea during a flare-up of ulcerative colitis.

Irritable Bowel Syndrome (IBS)

- **Description**: A common disorder affecting the large intestine, causing cramping, abdominal pain, bloating, gas, diarrhea, and constipation.
- **Priority Facts**: Not directly related to underlying bowel damage; often linked to stress and certain foods.
- **NCLEX Pearls**: Management includes dietary changes, stress reduction, and sometimes medication.
- **Top Safety Tips**: Educate about identifying and avoiding trigger foods and stress management techniques.
- **Sample Question**: What dietary recommendation is generally advised for patients with IBS?
- A. Strict gluten-free diet.
- B. High-protein, low-carbohydrate diet.
- C. Increasing dietary fiber intake gradually.
- D. Elimination of all dairy products.
- **Correct Answer**: C. Increasing dietary fiber intake gradually.
- **Rationale**: Gradually increasing fiber can help regulate bowel movements in IBS, but it should be done carefully to avoid excessive gas and bloating.

Gallstones

- **Description**: Hardened deposits in the gallbladder, often composed of cholesterol or bilirubin, that can cause pain and blockages.
- **Priority Facts**: Risk factors include obesity, high-fat diet, and rapid weight loss.
- **NCLEX Pearls**: Focus on dietary modifications to manage symptoms and prevent complications.
- **Top Safety Tips**: Monitor for signs of gallbladder inflammation or obstruction, such as severe abdominal pain and jaundice.

- **Sample Question**: What is an important dietary recommendation for a patient with gallstones?
- A. High-fat, low-carbohydrate diet.
- B. Low-fat, high-fiber diet.
- C. High-protein, high-calorie diet.
- D. Unrestricted, balanced diet with no specific modifications.
- **Correct Answer**: B. Low-fat, high-fiber diet.
- **Rationale**: A low-fat diet helps reduce gallbladder stimulation, thus decreasing the risk of gallstone-related symptoms and complications.

Hepatitis

- **Description**: Inflammation of the liver, often caused by viral infections (Hepatitis A, B, C), toxins, alcohol, and certain medications.
- **Priority Facts**: Symptoms may include jaundice, fatigue, and abdominal pain.
- **NCLEX Pearls**: Emphasize prevention through vaccination (for Hepatitis A and B) and safe practices.
- **Top Safety Tips**: Monitor liver function tests and educate about avoiding alcohol and hepatotoxic medications.
- **Sample Question**: What is a key nursing intervention for a patient with acute hepatitis?
- A. Encouraging alcohol consumption in moderation.
- B. Administering over-the-counter pain relievers as needed.
- C. Monitoring for signs of liver failure.
- D. Prescribing antiviral medications without a physician's order.
- **Correct Answer**: C. Monitoring for signs of liver failure.
- **Rationale**: Monitoring for liver failure is crucial in hepatitis as the disease can progress, causing severe liver damage.

Pancreatitis

- **Description**: Inflammation of the pancreas that can be acute or chronic, often related to gallstones or alcohol use.
- **Priority Facts**: Symptoms include severe upper abdominal pain, nausea, and vomiting.
- **NCLEX Pearls**: Management includes pain relief, fluid management, and nutritional support.
- **Top Safety Tips**: Monitor for complications such as infection, diabetes, and malabsorption.
- **Sample Question**: During an acute pancreatitis attack, what is the MOST appropriate nursing action?
- A. Encouraging large, frequent meals.
- B. Administering oral pancreatic enzymes.
- C. Providing adequate pain management and fluid replacement.
- D. Recommending increased alcohol intake to stimulate digestion.
- **Correct Answer**: C. Providing adequate pain management and fluid replacement.
- **Rationale**: Pain management and fluid replacement are critical in managing acute pancreatitis and preventing complications.

Gastroenteritis

- **Description**: Inflammation of the stomach and intestines, typically resulting from a viral or bacterial infection.
- **Priority Facts**: Common symptoms include diarrhea, vomiting, abdominal pain, and dehydration.
- **NCLEX Pearls**: Focus on hydration and electrolyte replacement, and prevention of transmission.
- **Top Safety Tips**: Monitor for dehydration and electrolyte imbalances, and educate about proper hand hygiene.
- **Sample Question**: What is a priority nursing action for a patient with gastroenteritis?

- A. Restricting all oral intake until symptoms resolve.
- B. Providing antidiarrheal medication after each loose stool.
- C. Encouraging clear fluids and oral rehydration solutions.
- D. Administering antibiotics without waiting for stool culture results.
- **Correct Answer**: C. Encouraging clear fluids and oral rehydration solutions.
- **Rationale**: Oral rehydration is essential in managing gastroenteritis to prevent dehydration and restore electrolyte balance.

Colorectal Cancer

- **Description**: Cancer that starts in the colon or rectum, often beginning as small, benign polyps that can become cancerous over time.
- **Priority Facts**: Risk factors include age, family history, high-fat diet, and a sedentary lifestyle.
- **NCLEX Pearls**: Emphasize the importance of regular screening and early detection.
- **Top Safety Tips**: Monitor for symptoms like changes in bowel habits, blood in the stool, and unexplained weight loss.
- **Sample Question**: What is the MOST effective way to prevent colorectal cancer?
- A. Consuming a high-fat diet.
- B. Regular colorectal screening starting at an appropriate age.
- C. Taking antibiotics as a preventive measure.
- D. Exercising only after the age of 50.
- **Correct Answer**: B. Regular colorectal screening starting at an appropriate age.
- **Rationale**: Regular screening is the most effective way to detect colorectal cancer early when it's most treatable.

Neurological System Disorders

Stroke

- **Description**: A medical emergency caused by interrupted or reduced blood supply to the brain, leading to brain cell death.
- **Priority Facts**: Types include ischemic (blockage) and hemorrhagic (bleeding). Recognizing symptoms (F.A.S.T.) is critical.
- **NCLEX Pearls**: Time is brain – immediate treatment is crucial.
- **Top Safety Tips**: Monitor neurological status, maintain airway patency, and manage blood pressure.
- **Sample Question**: What is the INITIAL nursing action for a patient suspected of having a stroke?
- A. Administer aspirin immediately.
- B. Start an IV infusion of normal saline.
- C. Conduct a thorough physical assessment.
- D. Ensure a CT scan of the head is performed urgently.
- **Correct Answer**: D. Ensure a CT scan of the head is performed urgently.
- **Rationale**: An urgent CT scan is needed to differentiate between ischemic and hemorrhagic stroke for appropriate treatment.

Alzheimer's Disease

- **Description**: A progressive neurological disorder that causes brain cells to waste away and die, leading to a decline in memory and mental function.
- **Priority Facts**: Most common cause of dementia among older adults.
- **NCLEX Pearls**: Focus on maintaining patient safety and supporting ADLs (Activities of Daily Living).
- **Top Safety Tips**: Create a safe environment to prevent injury and provide consistent, gentle orientation to reality.
- **Sample Question**: What is an essential strategy in the care of a patient with Alzheimer's Disease?
- A. Keeping the environment brightly lit at all times.
- B. Frequently reorienting the patient to time, place, and person.

- C. Implementing physical restraints to prevent wandering.
- D. Changing the room layout often to provide stimulation.
- **Correct Answer**: B. Frequently reorienting the patient to time, place, and person.
- **Rationale**: Regular orientation aids in maintaining cognitive function and reducing confusion in Alzheimer's patients.

Parkinson's Disease

- **Description**: A progressive nervous system disorder that affects movement, often including tremors, stiffness, and bradykinesia (slow movement).
- **Priority Facts**: The cause involves a decrease in dopamine levels.
- **NCLEX Pearls**: Management includes medication (e.g., Levodopa) and physical therapy.
- **Top Safety Tips**: Assist with ambulation, provide a safe environment, and monitor for swallowing difficulties.
- **Sample Question**: What nursing intervention is beneficial for a patient with Parkinson's Disease?
- A. Encourage rapid, complex movements to improve mobility.
- B. Provide small, frequent meals to facilitate easier swallowing.
- C. Isolate the patient to reduce the risk of infections.
- D. Administer dopamine antagonists to control tremors.
- **Correct Answer**: B. Provide small, frequent meals to facilitate easier swallowing.
- **Rationale**: Patients with Parkinson's often have difficulty swallowing; smaller, more manageable meals can help maintain nutrition and reduce choking risk.

Multiple Sclerosis

- **Description**: A chronic autoimmune disease involving damage to the sheaths of nerve cells in the brain and spinal cord, manifesting in a wide range of neurological symptoms.
- **Priority Facts**: Symptoms can include muscle weakness, lack of coordination, and visual disturbances.
- **NCLEX Pearls**: Treatment focuses on slowing disease progression and managing symptoms.
- **Top Safety Tips**: Monitor for mobility and sensory changes, and provide emotional and physical support.
- **Sample Question**: What is an important aspect of care for patients with Multiple Sclerosis?
- A. Encouraging intense exercise to combat muscle weakness.
- B. Administering corticosteroids during acute exacerbations.
- C. Restricting fluid intake to manage bladder dysfunction.
- D. Implementing a high-carbohydrate, low-protein diet.
- **Correct Answer**: B. Administering corticosteroids during acute exacerbations.
- **Rationale**: Corticosteroids can reduce nerve inflammation during MS flare-ups, temporarily improving symptoms.

Epilepsy

- **Description**: A central nervous system disorder in which brain activity becomes abnormal, causing seizures or periods of unusual behavior, sensations, and sometimes loss of awareness.
- **Priority Facts**: Can have various causes, including genetic influence, head trauma, and brain conditions.
- **NCLEX Pearls**: Seizure management and prevention are key.
- **Top Safety Tips**: Ensure a safe environment to prevent injury during seizures and administer antiepileptic drugs as prescribed.
- **Sample Question**: What is a priority nursing action during a seizure?

- A. Restrain the patient to prevent injury.
- B. Insert a tongue depressor to prevent biting the tongue.
- C. Clear the area around the patient and protect the head.
- D. Offer water to the patient to prevent dehydration.
- **Correct Answer**: C. Clear the area around the patient and protect the head.
- **Rationale**: Protecting the patient from injury during a seizure is crucial. This includes clearing the surrounding area and providing head protection.

Migraines and Other Types of Headaches

- **Description**: Migraines are a type of headache characterized by intense, throbbing pain often accompanied by nausea, vomiting, and sensitivity to light and sound. Other types include tension and cluster headaches.
- **Priority Facts**: Triggers can vary widely, including stress, certain foods, hormonal changes, and environmental factors.
- **NCLEX Pearls**: Treatment includes both preventive measures and acute symptom management.
- **Top Safety Tips**: Educate patients about identifying and avoiding triggers, and proper medication use.
- **Sample Question**: What is a key intervention for a patient experiencing a migraine?
- A. Encourage caffeine consumption to constrict blood vessels.
- B. Provide a quiet, dark room and administer prescribed medication.
- C. Advise vigorous physical activity to increase endorphin levels.
- D. Recommend watching television or reading to distract from the pain.
- **Correct Answer**: B. Provide a quiet, dark room and administer prescribed medication.
- **Rationale**: A quiet, dark room can help reduce migraine symptoms, and administering prescribed medication can help alleviate pain and other symptoms.

Amyotrophic Lateral Sclerosis (ALS)

- **Description**: A progressive neurodegenerative disease affecting nerve cells in the brain and spinal cord, leading to muscle weakness and atrophy.
- **Priority Facts**: No cure currently exists, and treatment focuses on symptom management and maintaining quality of life.
- **NCLEX Pearls**: Monitor for respiratory compromise and difficulty in swallowing.
- **Top Safety Tips**: Provide adaptive equipment for mobility and communication, and ensure nutritional needs are met.
- **Sample Question**: What is an important aspect of care for a patient with ALS?
- A. Implementing passive range-of-motion exercises to maintain muscle tone.
- B. Preparing for curative surgical interventions.
- C. Encouraging independent feeding and ambulation for as long as possible.
- D. Regular use of muscle relaxants to prevent muscle spasms.
- **Correct Answer**: A. Implementing passive range-of-motion exercises to maintain muscle tone.
- **Rationale**: Passive range-of-motion exercises can help maintain joint flexibility and reduce the risk of contractures in ALS patients.

Meningitis

- **Description**: Inflammation of the protective membranes covering the brain and spinal cord, typically caused by infection.
- **Priority Facts**: Symptoms include severe headache, fever, neck stiffness, and sensitivity to light.
- **NCLEX Pearls**: Early diagnosis and treatment are crucial. Isolation precautions may be necessary for bacterial meningitis.
- **Top Safety Tips**: Monitor for signs of increased intracranial pressure

and administer antibiotics as prescribed for bacterial meningitis.
- **Sample Question**: What is the FIRST nursing action for a patient suspected of having meningitis?
- A. Administer a steroid to reduce inflammation.
- B. Initiate seizure precautions.
- C. Obtain blood cultures and start empirical antibiotic therapy.
- D. Perform a lumbar puncture immediately.
- **Correct Answer**: C. Obtain blood cultures and start empirical antibiotic therapy.
- **Rationale**: Obtaining blood cultures and starting empirical antibiotic therapy are essential in managing bacterial meningitis, even before confirming the diagnosis.

Peripheral Neuropathy

- **Description**: A result of damage to the peripheral nerves, often causing weakness, numbness, and pain, typically in the hands and feet.
- **Priority Facts**: Common causes include diabetes, infections, and exposure to toxins.
- **NCLEX Pearls**: Focus on managing underlying conditions and symptom relief.
- **Top Safety Tips**: Educate about foot care, monitor for skin injuries, and ensure safety in the presence of sensory deficits.
- **Sample Question**: What is a key nursing intervention for a patient with peripheral neuropathy?
- A. Encourage walking barefoot for increased foot strength.
- B. Regularly inspect feet for injuries and changes.
- C. Apply heat packs to numb areas frequently.
- D. Recommend high-impact exercises to improve circulation.
- **Correct Answer**: B. Regularly inspect feet for injuries and changes.
- **Rationale**: Due to reduced sensation, patients with peripheral neuropathy may not notice injuries, making regular foot inspections crucial for preventing complications.

Traumatic Brain Injury (TBI)

- **Description**: A form of brain injury caused by a bump, blow, or jolt to the head that disrupts normal brain function.
- **Priority Facts**: Severity ranges from mild (concussion) to severe, with lasting effects on physical and cognitive abilities.
- **NCLEX Pearls**: Monitor for changes in neurological status and signs of increased intracranial pressure.
- **Top Safety Tips**: Provide a safe environment to prevent falls, and closely monitor airway and vital signs.
- **Sample Question**: In the acute phase of a moderate to severe TBI, what is the priority nursing action?
- A. Encourage cognitive stimulation through conversation and reading.
- B. Keep the patient in a supine position to increase cerebral perfusion.
- C. Monitor for signs of increased intracranial pressure.
- D. Administer diuretics to decrease intracranial fluid volume.
- **Correct Answer**: C. Monitor for signs of increased intracranial pressure.
- **Rationale**: Monitoring for increased intracranial pressure is critical in managing TBI to prevent secondary brain injury.

Musculoskeletal System Disorders

Osteoarthritis

- **Description**: A degenerative joint disease characterized by the breakdown of cartilage and underlying bone, leading to pain and stiffness, primarily in the hips, knees, and hands.
- **Priority Facts**: Most common form of arthritis, associated with aging and wear and tear of joints.
- **NCLEX Pearls**: Pain management and maintaining joint function are key.
- **Top Safety Tips**: Encourage gentle exercises like swimming or walking, and use of assistive devices as needed.
- **Sample Question**: What is an effective nursing intervention for managing

a patient with osteoarthritis?
- A. Advising complete bed rest to avoid joint strain.
- B. Administering high-impact aerobic exercises.
- C. Recommending regular, gentle physical activity.
- D. Applying cold compresses exclusively for pain relief.
- **Correct Answer**: C. Recommending regular, gentle physical activity.
- **Rationale**: Regular, gentle exercises help maintain joint flexibility and muscle strength in osteoarthritis without causing excessive wear.

Rheumatoid Arthritis

- **Description**: A chronic inflammatory disorder affecting many joints, including those in the hands and feet, characterized by joint swelling, pain, and stiffness.
- **Priority Facts**: It's an autoimmune disorder that can cause joint deformity and bone erosion.
- **NCLEX Pearls**: Early and aggressive treatment can help manage symptoms and prevent joint damage.
- **Top Safety Tips**: Monitor for side effects of medication and encourage activities that reduce joint stress.
- **Sample Question**: What is important to include in the care plan for a patient with rheumatoid arthritis?
- A. Encouraging heavy weight lifting for strengthening.
- B. Regular application of hot and cold treatments to affected joints.
- C. Immobilizing affected joints in a fixed position.
- D. Focusing solely on pharmacological interventions.
- **Correct Answer**: B. Regular application of hot and cold treatments to affected joints.
- **Rationale**: Alternating hot and cold treatments can help reduce joint pain and inflammation in rheumatoid arthritis.

Osteoporosis

- **Description**: A bone disease that occurs when the body loses too much bone, makes too little bone, or both, leading to weak and brittle bones.
- **Priority Facts**: Common in older adults, especially postmenopausal women, and can lead to fractures.
- **NCLEX Pearls**: Focus on fall prevention, adequate calcium and vitamin D intake, and regular bone density tests.
- **Top Safety Tips**: Encourage weight-bearing exercises and educate about medication adherence.
- **Sample Question**: What is a primary nursing goal for the care of a patient with osteoporosis?
- A. Encouraging high-impact sports to strengthen bones.
- B. Administering bisphosphonates intravenously daily.
- C. Promoting activities that prevent falls and fractures.
- D. Limiting fluid intake to reduce the risk of bone swelling.
- **Correct Answer**: C. Promoting activities that prevent falls and fractures.
- **Rationale**: Preventing falls is crucial in osteoporosis to reduce the risk of fractures due to bone fragility.

Gout

- **Description**: A form of arthritis characterized by severe pain, redness, and tenderness in joints, particularly the big toe, caused by crystallization of uric acid.
- **Priority Facts**: Risk factors include diet (high in purine), obesity, and certain medical conditions.
- **NCLEX Pearls**: Management includes dietary modifications, medications, and avoiding triggers like alcohol.
- **Top Safety Tips**: Educate about avoiding foods high in purines and the importance of medication compliance.
- **Sample Question**: What dietary modification is MOST recommended for a patient with gout?

- A. Increasing protein intake, particularly red meats.
- B. High intake of purine-rich foods like shellfish and alcohol.
- C. Drinking plenty of fluids and avoiding high-purine foods.
- D. A strict vegetarian diet with no protein.
- **Correct Answer**: C. Drinking plenty of fluids and avoiding high-purine foods.
- **Rationale**: Hydration helps eliminate uric acid from the body, and avoiding high-purine foods reduces the risk of gout flare-ups.

Fibromyalgia

- **Description**: A chronic condition characterized by widespread musculoskeletal pain accompanied by fatigue, sleep, memory, and mood issues.
- **Priority Facts**: Causes are unknown, but it's thought to be related to pain signal processing in the brain.
- **NCLEX Pearls**: Treatment is symptomatic, focusing on pain management, improving sleep, and exercise.
- **Top Safety Tips**: Encourage regular low-impact exercise and stress reduction techniques.
- **Sample Question**: What intervention is beneficial for a patient with fibromyalgia?
- A. Vigorous exercise to improve muscle tone.
- B. Prolonged bed rest to reduce fatigue.
- C. Gentle aerobic exercises and adequate rest.
- D. High-dose opioid medications for chronic pain.
- **Correct Answer**: C. Gentle aerobic exercises and adequate rest.
- **Rationale**: Gentle exercises, like walking or swimming, can help manage pain and fatigue in fibromyalgia, while adequate rest helps manage symptoms.

Muscular Dystrophy

- **Description**: A group of genetic diseases characterized by progressive weakness and loss of muscle mass.
- **Priority Facts**: Different types affect various muscle groups and have varying degrees of severity.
- **NCLEX Pearls**: No cure; focus on maximizing patient function and quality of life.
- **Top Safety Tips**: Provide assistance with mobility, monitor respiratory function, and support nutritional needs.
- **Sample Question**: What is a crucial nursing intervention for a patient with muscular dystrophy?
- A. Encouraging independent ambulation at all times.
- B. Implementing passive range-of-motion exercises daily.
- C. Restricting all physical activities to conserve energy.
- D. Administering high-dose corticosteroids as a curative treatment.
- **Correct Answer**: B. Implementing passive range-of-motion exercises daily.
- **Rationale**: Passive range-of-motion exercises help maintain joint flexibility and reduce the risk of contractures in patients with muscular dystrophy.

Tendonitis

- **Description**: Inflammation or irritation of a tendon, often caused by overuse or injury.
- **Priority Facts**: Common in the wrists, elbows, shoulders, and knees.
- **NCLEX Pearls**: Treatment includes rest, ice, and over-the-counter pain relievers.
- **Top Safety Tips**: Educate about proper technique in repetitive tasks and the importance of regular breaks.
- **Sample Question**: What is an effective nursing intervention for a patient with tendonitis?

- A. Encouraging intense exercise to strengthen the tendon.
- B. Applying ice packs to the affected area for pain relief.
- C. Recommending complete immobilization of the affected limb.
- D. Prescribing antibiotics as a standard treatment.
- **Correct Answer**: B. Applying ice packs to the affected area for pain relief.
- **Rationale**: Ice packs can help reduce inflammation and pain in tendonitis.

Bursitis

- **Description**: Inflammation of the bursae, small fluid-filled sacs that cushion the bones, tendons, and muscles near the joints.
- **Priority Facts**: Commonly affects the shoulder, elbow, and hip.
- **NCLEX Pearls**: Similar to tendonitis, treatment includes rest, ice, and pain management.
- **Top Safety Tips**: Encourage gentle range-of-motion exercises and use of assistive devices if needed.
- **Sample Question**: What is an important self-care measure for a patient with bursitis of the shoulder?
- A. Lifting heavy weights with the affected arm.
- B. Resting the joint and avoiding repetitive movements.
- C. Keeping the shoulder completely immobile for several weeks.
- D. Applying heat continuously for the first 48 hours.
- **Correct Answer**: B. Resting the joint and avoiding repetitive movements.
- **Rationale**: Resting the affected joint and avoiding activities that worsen the condition are key in managing bursitis.

Lupus

- **Description**: An autoimmune disease that causes inflammation and a wide range of symptoms across different body systems.
- **Priority Facts**: Symptoms are often nonspecific and may include fatigue, joint pain, rash, and fever.
- **NCLEX Pearls**: Management is highly individualized, focusing on symp-

tom control and preventing flare-ups.
- **Top Safety Tips**: Monitor for signs of organ involvement and educate about sun protection.
- **Sample Question**: What is a critical aspect of managing a patient with lupus?
- A. Avoiding all physical activity to prevent fatigue.
- B. Administering immunosuppressive medication as prescribed.
- C. Applying cold compresses to rashes daily.
- D. Increasing exposure to sunlight to improve mood.
- **Correct Answer**: B. Administering immunosuppressive medication as prescribed.
- **Rationale**: Immunosuppressive medications are often used in lupus to control the immune system and prevent flares.

Back Pain (e.g., Herniated Disc)

- **Description**: Pain in the back area, which can be acute or chronic; a herniated disc involves a problem with the rubbery disc between spinal bones.
- **Priority Facts**: Causes of back pain vary, including muscle or ligament strain, bulging or ruptured discs, arthritis, or skeletal irregularities.
- **NCLEX Pearls**: Focus on pain relief, physical therapy, and maintaining activity as tolerated.
- **Top Safety Tips**: Educate about proper body mechanics and encourage exercises to strengthen back muscles.
- **Sample Question**: What is a recommended initial intervention for acute lower back pain from a herniated disc?
- A. Extended bed rest for several weeks.
- B. Starting high-intensity weight lifting immediately.
- C. Applying heat or ice to the affected area and taking pain relievers.
- D. Undergoing immediate surgery as a first-line treatment.
- **Correct Answer**: C. Applying heat or ice to the affected area and taking pain relievers.

- **Rationale**: Heat or ice can help reduce pain and muscle spasms in acute lower back pain, and over-the-counter pain relievers can also be helpful.

Endocrine System Disorders

Diabetes Mellitus (Type 1 and Type 2)

- **Description**: A chronic condition where the body is unable to properly use and store glucose. Type 1 is characterized by the body's failure to produce insulin, while Type 2 involves insulin resistance.
- **Priority Facts**: Key elements include blood sugar monitoring, insulin therapy (Type 1), oral hypoglycemics (Type 2), diet, and exercise.
- **NCLEX Pearls**: Recognize symptoms of hypo- and hyperglycemia and understand insulin administration.
- **Top Safety Tips**: Educate about consistent carbohydrate intake, regular blood glucose monitoring, and proper medication use.
- **Sample Question**: What is essential when educating a patient with newly diagnosed Type 1 diabetes mellitus?
- A. Advising to stop insulin if blood sugar is under 200 mg/dL.
- B. Demonstrating how to self-administer insulin injections.
- C. Recommending an unrestricted diet to maintain weight.
- D. Suggesting oral hypoglycemic agents instead of insulin.
- **Correct Answer**: B. Demonstrating how to self-administer insulin injections.
- **Rationale**: Self-administration of insulin is a critical skill for managing Type 1 diabetes, as these patients require daily insulin for survival.

Hyperthyroidism (e.g., Graves' Disease)

- **Description**: An overactive thyroid gland producing excessive amounts of thyroid hormones, leading to symptoms like rapid heart rate, weight loss, and nervousness.
- **Priority Facts**: Graves' Disease is a common cause, characterized by an

autoimmune response.
- **NCLEX Pearls**: Management includes antithyroid medications, radioactive iodine therapy, or surgery.
- **Top Safety Tips**: Monitor cardiac status and educate about the signs of thyrotoxicosis.
- **Sample Question**: What is a priority nursing intervention for a patient with hyperthyroidism?
- A. Encouraging vigorous exercise to reduce nervous energy.
- B. Administering thyroid hormone replacement.
- C. Monitoring heart rate and rhythm.
- D. Recommending a high-calorie diet to counteract weight loss.
- **Correct Answer**: C. Monitoring heart rate and rhythm.
- **Rationale**: Cardiac monitoring is important in hyperthyroidism due to the risk of tachycardia and other arrhythmias.

Hypothyroidism (e.g., Hashimoto's Thyroiditis)

- **Description**: An underactive thyroid gland leading to inadequate production of thyroid hormones, causing symptoms like fatigue, weight gain, and cold intolerance.
- **Priority Facts**: Hashimoto's Thyroiditis is a common cause, where the immune system attacks the thyroid.
- **NCLEX Pearls**: Treatment involves thyroid hormone replacement therapy.
- **Top Safety Tips**: Monitor for medication side effects and educate about the importance of lifelong therapy.
- **Sample Question**: What is important to include in patient education for hypothyroidism?
- A. Taking thyroid medication only when symptoms are severe.
- B. Understanding the lifelong need for thyroid hormone replacement.
- C. Increasing iodine intake as the sole treatment method.
- D. Stopping medication if experiencing initial side effects.
- **Correct Answer**: B. Understanding the lifelong need for thyroid hormone

replacement.
- **Rationale**: Lifelong thyroid hormone replacement is typically required in hypothyroidism to maintain normal metabolic function.

Cushing's Syndrome

- **Description**: A condition resulting from prolonged exposure to high levels of cortisol, leading to symptoms like weight gain, thinning skin, and easy bruising.
- **Priority Facts**: Can result from long-term use of corticosteroid medication or the body producing too much cortisol.
- **NCLEX Pearls**: Treatment depends on the cause but may include surgery, radiation, medication, or gradual reduction of corticosteroid use.
- **Top Safety Tips**: Monitor for signs of infection, glucose levels, and changes in mental status.
- **Sample Question**: What is a key nursing consideration for a patient with Cushing's Syndrome?
- A. Restricting fluid intake to manage edema.
- B. Monitoring for signs of infection and hyperglycemia.
- C. Encouraging high-impact exercises to strengthen bones.
- D. Applying tight bandages over bruised areas.
- **Correct Answer**: B. Monitoring for signs of infection and hyperglycemia.
- **Rationale**: Patients with Cushing's Syndrome are at increased risk for infections and may develop hyperglycemia due to the effects of cortisol on glucose metabolism.

Addison's Disease

- **Description**: A disorder in which the adrenal glands produce insufficient amounts of certain hormones, such as cortisol and aldosterone.
- **Priority Facts**: Symptoms include fatigue, weight loss, low blood pressure, and darkening of the skin.
- **NCLEX Pearls**: Lifelong hormone replacement therapy is necessary.

- **Top Safety Tips**: Monitor for signs of adrenal crisis, such as severe vomiting, diarrhea, and hypotension.
- **Sample Question**: What is a crucial aspect of managing a patient with Addison's Disease?
- A. Increasing sodium intake during periods of stress.
- B. Administering corticosteroid replacement therapy as prescribed.
- C. Encouraging the discontinuation of medications during periods of illness.
- D. Limiting fluid intake to prevent water retention.
- **Correct Answer**: B. Administering corticosteroid replacement therapy as prescribed.
- **Rationale**: Corticosteroid replacement is essential in Addison's Disease to compensate for the underproduction of adrenal hormones and prevent an adrenal crisis.

Polycystic Ovary Syndrome (PCOS)

- **Description**: A hormonal disorder causing enlarged ovaries with small cysts on the outer edges.
- **Priority Facts**: Common symptoms include menstrual irregularity, excess hair growth, acne, and obesity.
- **NCLEX Pearls**: Managing PCOS involves lifestyle changes, such as diet and exercise, and medications like metformin.
- **Top Safety Tips**: Monitor for complications such as diabetes and cardiovascular disease.
- **Sample Question**: What lifestyle modification is MOST effective for managing symptoms in a patient with PCOS?
- A. High carbohydrate, low-fat diet.
- B. Regular physical exercise and healthy diet.
- C. Strict bed rest to conserve energy.
- D. Avoiding all forms of hormonal medication.
- **Correct Answer**: B. Regular physical exercise and healthy diet.
- **Rationale**: Exercise and a healthy diet can help manage weight and reduce

the symptoms and long-term risks associated with PCOS.

Hyperparathyroidism

- **Description**: Excess production of parathyroid hormone by the parathyroid glands, affecting calcium levels.
- **Priority Facts**: Can lead to osteoporosis, kidney stones, and neuromuscular symptoms.
- **NCLEX Pearls**: Treatment may include surgery, medications, and monitoring of calcium levels.
- **Top Safety Tips**: Monitor for signs of hypercalcemia and kidney dysfunction.
- **Sample Question**: What is a crucial aspect of managing a patient with hyperparathyroidism?
- A. Encouraging a high-calcium diet.
- B. Administering calcium supplements.
- C. Monitoring serum calcium and renal function.
- D. Limiting fluid intake to reduce the risk of kidney stones.
- **Correct Answer**: C. Monitoring serum calcium and renal function.
- **Rationale**: Monitoring calcium levels and renal function is essential in managing hyperparathyroidism to prevent complications.

Pituitary Disorders (e.g., Pituitary Tumors)

- **Description**: Conditions affecting the pituitary gland, ranging from benign tumors to hormone deficiencies or excesses.
- **Priority Facts**: Symptoms vary depending on whether the tumor is functional (hormone-secreting) or non-functional.
- **NCLEX Pearls**: Treatment may include medication, hormone replacement, or surgery.
- **Top Safety Tips**: Monitor for changes in vision, headache, and signs of hormonal imbalances.
- **Sample Question**: What is an important nursing intervention for a

patient with a pituitary tumor?
- A. Regularly assessing for changes in visual acuity and field.
- B. Encouraging increased salt intake to manage hyponatremia.
- C. Frequent high-intensity exercise to reduce tumor size.
- D. Administration of anticoagulant therapy as a standard treatment.
- **Correct Answer**: A. Regularly assessing for changes in visual acuity and field.
- **Rationale**: Pituitary tumors can impact vision due to their proximity to the optic nerves; thus, regular eye exams are important.

Acromegaly

- **Description**: A disorder caused by excessive secretion of growth hormone, usually due to a benign tumor on the pituitary gland.
- **Priority Facts**: Characterized by enlarged bones in the hands, feet, and face.
- **NCLEX Pearls**: Treatment includes surgery, medication, and radiation therapy.
- **Top Safety Tips**: Monitor for complications such as diabetes, hypertension, and heart disease.
- **Sample Question**: What is a key component of care for a patient with acromegaly?
- A. Encouraging a high-calcium diet to promote bone growth.
- B. Monitoring for signs of diabetes and cardiovascular disease.
- C. Applying topical creams to reduce skin thickening.
- D. Recommending bed rest to slow the progression.
- **Correct Answer**: B. Monitoring for signs of diabetes and cardiovascular disease.
- **Rationale**: Due to the hormonal imbalances in acromegaly, patients are at higher risk for diabetes and cardiovascular disease.

Osteoporosis

- **Description**: A bone disease characterized by decreased density and quality of bone, leading to fragility and increased risk of fractures.
- **Priority Facts**: Common in postmenopausal women and older adults, often related to low calcium and vitamin D levels, and reduced physical activity.
- **NCLEX Pearls**: Prevention and treatment include calcium and vitamin D supplementation, and weight-bearing exercises.
- **Top Safety Tips**: Educate about fall prevention and adherence to bone health medications.
- **Sample Question**: What intervention is MOST effective in preventing osteoporosis in at-risk populations?
- A. Prolonged bed rest to prevent bone stress.
- B. High-dose corticosteroid therapy.
- C. Regular weight-bearing exercises and adequate calcium intake.
- D. Limiting all physical activities to reduce the risk of fractures.
- **Correct Answer**: C. Regular weight-bearing exercises and adequate calcium intake.
- **Rationale**: Weight-bearing exercises strengthen bones, and adequate calcium intake is essential for bone health, both of which are crucial in preventing osteoporosis.

Renal and Urinary System Disorders

Chronic Kidney Disease (CKD)

- **Description:** A progressive loss of kidney function over time, leading to the accumulation of waste products and fluid imbalances.
- **Priority Facts:** Monitoring renal function tests, understanding stages of CKD, and managing comorbid conditions like hypertension and diabetes.
- **NCLEX Pearls:** Focus on early detection through screening in high-risk populations and slowing progression with strict blood pressure and blood

sugar control.
- **Top Safety Tips:** Regularly monitor electrolyte levels, fluid status, and signs of uremia; manage medications carefully, considering altered renal clearance.
- **Sample Question:** What is a key nursing consideration when caring for a patient with advanced Chronic Kidney Disease (CKD)? A. Encourage high protein intake. B. Monitor for signs of fluid overload. C. Limit all fluid intake to 500 mL/day. D. Administer over-the-counter NSAIDs for pain management.
- **Correct Answer:** B. Monitor for signs of fluid overload.
- **Rationale:** Patients with advanced CKD often have reduced urine output and are at risk for fluid overload. Monitoring for signs like edema, hypertension, and lung crackles is crucial. Limiting protein intake (not increasing it), avoiding NSAIDs due to nephrotoxicity, and managing fluid restrictions based on individual needs are also key.

Urinary Tract Infections (UTIs)

- **Description:** Infections of the urinary system, most commonly involving the bladder and urethra.
- **Priority Facts:** Recognizing symptoms like dysuria and urgency, understanding the higher prevalence in females, and identifying risk factors such as indwelling catheters.
- **NCLEX Pearls:** Emphasize the importance of proper perineal hygiene and adequate fluid intake for prevention.
- **Top Safety Tips:** Ensure clean technique with catheter insertions and timely removal of catheters to reduce infection risk.
- **Sample Question:** Which intervention is MOST effective in preventing hospital-acquired urinary tract infections (UTIs)? A. Limiting fluid intake during the night. B. Frequent bladder scanning for all patients. C. Aseptic insertion and care of urinary catheters. D. Administering prophylactic antibiotics routinely.
- **Correct Answer:** C. Aseptic insertion and care of urinary catheters.

- **Rationale:** Maintaining aseptic technique during catheter insertion and ensuring proper ongoing care are crucial to prevent UTIs, especially catheter-associated UTIs. Prophylactic antibiotics are not routinely recommended, as they can contribute to resistance.

Kidney Stones

- **Description:** Hard mineral and salt deposits that form in the kidneys and can cause severe pain and urinary complications.
- **Priority Facts:** Recognizing symptoms like severe flank pain and hematuria, understanding dietary and hydration factors in prevention.
- **NCLEX Pearls:** Focus on pain management, hydration strategies, and dietary modifications depending on stone type.
- **Top Safety Tips:** Monitor for urinary obstruction signs and encourage fluid intake to promote stone passage.
- **Sample Question:** A patient with a history of calcium oxalate kidney stones should be advised to: A. Increase intake of spinach and nuts. B. Limit fluid intake to reduce urinary output. C. Avoid high-oxalate foods and stay well hydrated. D. Consume more dairy products to bind with oxalate.
- **Correct Answer:** C. Avoid high-oxalate foods and stay well hydrated.
- **Rationale:** Patients with calcium oxalate stones should avoid high-oxalate foods like spinach and nuts. Increasing hydration helps prevent stone formation. Limiting fluids and consuming more dairy are not recommended in this scenario.

Glomerulonephritis

- **Description:** Inflammation of the tiny filters in the kidneys (glomeruli), often due to infection or an autoimmune process.
- **Priority Facts:** Understanding symptoms such as hematuria, proteinuria, and edema; awareness of post-streptococcal glomerulonephritis.
- **NCLEX Pearls:** Focus on early detection of renal impairment and manag-

ing underlying causes like infections.
- **Top Safety Tips:** Monitor renal function and fluid balance vigilantly, and manage blood pressure effectively.
- **Sample Question:** A patient with acute post-streptococcal glomerulonephritis is MOST likely to present with: A. Hypertension and hematuria. B. Severe abdominal pain and vomiting. C. Jaundice and dark urine. D. Hyperglycemia and polyuria.
- **Correct Answer:** A. Hypertension and hematuria.
- **Rationale:** Acute glomerulonephritis typically presents with hypertension (due to fluid retention) and hematuria (blood in the urine) due to glomerular damage. Jaundice, abdominal pain, hyperglycemia, and polyuria are not typical symptoms of this condition.

Polycystic Kidney Disease (PKD)

- **Description:** A genetic disorder characterized by the growth of numerous cysts in the kidneys.
- **Priority Facts:** Recognizing signs like hypertension, abdominal pain, and kidney infections; understanding genetic implications.
- **NCLEX Pearls:** Emphasize monitoring kidney function, controlling blood pressure, and recognizing complications.
- **Top Safety Tips:** Regularly assess for flank pain, changes in urinary patterns, and signs of infection or renal impairment.
- **Sample Question:** The nurse recognizes that a patient with polycystic kidney disease (PKD) is at increased risk for: A. Hyponatremia. B. Hypertension. C. Hypoglycemia. D. Hypercalcemia.
- **Correct Answer:** B. Hypertension.
- **Rationale:** Hypertension is a common complication of PKD due to the increased activity of the renin-angiotensin-aldosterone system and fluid retention related to reduced kidney function. The other options are not directly associated with PKD.

Urinary Incontinence

- **Description:** Involuntary leakage of urine due to various factors affecting bladder control.
- **Priority Facts:** Includes stress, urge, overflow, and functional incontinence. Common in older adults and postpartum women.
- **NCLEX Pearls:** Focus on differentiating types of incontinence for appropriate management strategies.
- **Top Safety Tips:** Implement bladder training techniques, encourage pelvic floor exercises, and use protective garments as necessary.
- **Sample Question:** What is an appropriate nursing intervention for a patient with stress urinary incontinence? A. Scheduled toileting every 2 hours. B. Pelvic floor muscle exercises (Kegel exercises). C. Intermittent catheterization. D. Administration of anticholinergic medication.
- **Correct Answer:** B. Pelvic floor muscle exercises (Kegel exercises).
- **Rationale:** Kegel exercises strengthen the pelvic floor muscles and are effective in managing stress urinary incontinence. Scheduled toileting is more for urge incontinence, intermittent catheterization is for overflow incontinence, and anticholinergics are used in urge incontinence.

Acute Kidney Injury (AKI)

- **Description:** A sudden decline in kidney function, leading to the accumulation of waste products and fluid imbalances.
- **Priority Facts:** Can be caused by decreased renal perfusion, direct kidney damage, or urinary tract obstructions.
- **NCLEX Pearls:** Monitor renal function tests, fluid status, and electrolyte levels closely.
- **Top Safety Tips:** Identify and treat the underlying cause, ensure adequate hydration, and avoid nephrotoxic agents.
- **Sample Question:** A patient with Acute Kidney Injury (AKI) is most likely to exhibit which laboratory finding? A. Decreased serum creatinine. B. Increased blood urea nitrogen (BUN). C. Decreased serum potassium. D. Increased urine output.
- **Correct Answer:** B. Increased blood urea nitrogen (BUN).

- **Rationale:** AKI commonly causes an increase in BUN due to the kidney's reduced ability to excrete urea. Decreased serum creatinine and increased urine output are not typical findings in AKI. Hyperkalemia, not hypokalemia, may occur due to decreased renal excretion.

Bladder Cancer

- **Description:** A malignancy arising in the urinary bladder lining, often presenting with hematuria.
- **Priority Facts:** Risk factors include smoking, exposure to certain chemicals, and chronic bladder inflammation.
- **NCLEX Pearls:** Emphasize early detection through hematuria screening in at-risk populations.
- **Top Safety Tips:** Monitor for changes in urinary patterns and signs of urinary tract infections, provide postoperative care for patients undergoing bladder surgery.
- **Sample Question:** Which symptom is MOST commonly associated with bladder cancer? A. Nocturia. B. Hematuria. C. Urinary urgency. D. Polyuria.
- **Correct Answer:** B. Hematuria.
- **Rationale:** Hematuria, or blood in the urine, is the most common and often the earliest sign of bladder cancer. The other symptoms can be associated but are not as specific as hematuria for bladder cancer.

Interstitial Cystitis (Painful Bladder Syndrome)

- **Description:** A chronic condition characterized by bladder pressure and pain and, frequently, urinary frequency.
- **Priority Facts:** Etiology is unknown, more common in women, and often associated with other chronic pain disorders.
- **NCLEX Pearls:** Focus on symptom management and patient education about lifestyle modifications.
- **Top Safety Tips:** Encourage dietary modifications, bladder training, and

stress management techniques.
- **Sample Question:** Which intervention is commonly used to manage Interstitial Cystitis (Painful Bladder Syndrome)? A. Regularly scheduled diuretics. B. Bladder instillations. C. Long-term antibiotic therapy. D. High fluid intake before bedtime.
- **Correct Answer:** B. Bladder instillations.
- **Rationale:** Bladder instillations with a solution that coats the bladder lining can reduce pain and frequency symptoms associated with interstitial cystitis. Diuretics and high fluid intake at night may exacerbate symptoms, and long-term antibiotics are not a standard treatment.

Prostate Disorders (e.g., Benign Prostatic Hyperplasia)

- **Description:** Enlargement of the prostate gland, common in older men, causing urinary symptoms.
- **Priority Facts:** Symptoms include difficulty starting urination, weak stream, and nocturia.
- **NCLEX Pearls:** Differentiate between benign and malignant prostate conditions. Focus on conservative management and medication therapy.
- **Top Safety Tips:** Monitor urinary output, educate about medications like alpha-blockers, and encourage regular follow-up.
- **Sample Question:** A nurse is educating a patient with Benign Prostatic Hyperplasia (BPH) about lifestyle modifications. Which advice should the nurse include? A. Limit fluid intake in the evening. B. Increase caffeine and alcohol consumption. C. Perform Kegel exercises twice daily. D. Take over-the-counter cold medications as needed.
- **Correct Answer:** A. Limit fluid intake in the evening.
- **Rationale:** Limiting fluid intake in the evening can help reduce nocturia, a common symptom of BPH. Caffeine and alcohol can exacerbate symptoms, Kegel exercises are not typically used for BPH management, and some OTC cold medications can worsen BPH symptoms.

Integumentary System Disorders

Acne

- **Description**: A skin condition characterized by the presence of pimples, blackheads, and cysts, primarily on the face, chest, and back.
- **Priority Facts**: Commonly occurs in adolescence but can persist into adulthood. Caused by clogged pores due to oil, dead skin, or bacteria.
- **NCLEX Pearls**: Treatment includes topical medications, oral antibiotics, and in severe cases, isotretinoin.
- **Top Safety Tips**: Educate about gentle skin care and avoiding picking or squeezing pimples.
- **Sample Question**: What is an important nursing instruction for a patient using topical acne treatments?
- A. Use abrasive scrubs daily to clear pores.
- B. Apply a thick layer of medication for best results.
- C. Avoid excessive sun exposure and use sunscreen.
- D. Discontinue treatment if skin irritation occurs.
- **Correct Answer**: C. Avoid excessive sun exposure and use sunscreen.
- **Rationale**: Some acne medications can make skin more sensitive to sunlight, hence the importance of sun protection.

Psoriasis

- **Description**: A chronic autoimmune skin disease that speeds up the life cycle of skin cells, causing cells to build up rapidly on the surface of the skin.
- **Priority Facts**: Presents as red patches with silvery scales, often on the scalp, elbows, knees, and lower back.
- **NCLEX Pearls**: Treatments include topical therapies, phototherapy, and systemic medications.
- **Top Safety Tips**: Educate about skin care, trigger avoidance, and adherence to treatment.

- **Sample Question**: What is a recommended non-pharmacological intervention for a patient with psoriasis?
- A. Regular sunbathing for prolonged periods.
- B. Moisturizing regularly with fragrance-free lotions.
- C. Using harsh soaps to remove scales.
- D. Scratching lesions to remove scales.
- **Correct Answer**: B. Moisturizing regularly with fragrance-free lotions.
- **Rationale**: Regular moisturizing helps reduce dryness and itching associated with psoriasis.

Eczema (Dermatitis)

- **Description**: A group of conditions that cause inflammation, itchiness, redness, and skin rash.
- **Priority Facts**: Triggers include irritants, allergens, stress, and dry skin.
- **NCLEX Pearls**: Management includes avoiding triggers, moisturizing the skin, and using corticosteroid creams.
- **Top Safety Tips**: Instruct on skin care and the importance of avoiding scratching.
- **Sample Question**: What is a key component of managing care for a patient with eczema?
- A. Taking hot showers daily.
- B. Applying moisturizer to damp skin after bathing.
- C. Using perfumed lotions to soothe the skin.
- D. Wearing woolen clothing directly against the skin.
- **Correct Answer**: B. Applying moisturizer to damp skin after bathing.
- **Rationale**: Applying moisturizer to damp skin helps lock in moisture, which is beneficial for managing eczema.

Skin Cancer (e.g., Melanoma, Basal Cell Carcinoma)

- **Description**: Skin cancer, including melanoma and basal cell carcinoma, involves the abnormal growth of skin cells, often due to UV radiation exposure.
- **Priority Facts**: Melanoma is more aggressive than basal cell carcinoma. Early detection is key.
- **NCLEX Pearls**: Emphasize the importance of regular skin checks and protection against UV exposure.
- **Top Safety Tips**: Educate about the ABCDEs of melanoma and the use of sunscreen.
- **Sample Question**: What is the MOST important preventive measure for reducing the risk of skin cancer?
- A. Using a tanning bed instead of sunbathing.
- B. Regular application of broad-spectrum sunscreen.
- C. Applying baby oil to skin before going outdoors.
- D. Checking skin annually for changes.
- **Correct Answer**: B. Regular application of broad-spectrum sunscreen.
- **Rationale**: Consistent use of sunscreen helps protect the skin from harmful UV rays, reducing the risk of skin cancer.

Rosacea

- **Description**: A chronic skin condition causing redness and visible blood vessels, often with red, pus-filled bumps, primarily on the face.
- **Priority Facts**: Triggers include heat, stress, alcohol, and spicy foods.
- **NCLEX Pearls**: Treatment focuses on managing symptoms and avoiding triggers.
- **Top Safety Tips**: Educate about trigger avoidance and gentle skin care.
- **Sample Question**: What lifestyle modification is important for a patient diagnosed with rosacea?
- A. Regularly using a sauna to open pores.
- B. Avoiding triggers known to exacerbate symptoms.

- C. Applying topical steroids daily.
- D. Scrubbing the face vigorously to reduce oil buildup.
- **Correct Answer**: B. Avoiding triggers known to exacerbate symptoms.
- **Rationale**: Avoiding individual triggers, such as certain foods, weather conditions, and activities, can help manage and reduce rosacea flare-ups.

Cellulitis

- **Description:** A common, potentially serious bacterial skin infection, often appearing as a swollen, red area that is hot and tender to the touch.
- **Priority Facts:** Commonly caused by Streptococcus and Staphylococcus bacteria; risk factors include skin breaks, chronic skin conditions, and compromised immune systems.
- **NCLEX Pearls:** Early recognition and treatment are key to preventing systemic spread.
- **Top Safety Tips:** Keep skin clean and dry, promptly treat any cuts or abrasions, and monitor for signs of infection.
- **Sample Question:** The MOST important nursing intervention for a patient with cellulitis of the lower leg is: A. Applying a warm, moist compress to the affected area. B. Encouraging high-intensity exercise to improve blood flow. C. Administering insulin for blood sugar control. D. Keeping the affected limb elevated.
- **Correct Answer:** D. Keeping the affected limb elevated.
- **Rationale:** Elevation of the affected limb helps reduce swelling and pain associated with cellulitis. Warm compresses can be beneficial, but elevation is a priority intervention. High-intensity exercise is not recommended, and insulin administration is specific to diabetic patients.

Herpes Zoster (Shingles)

- **Description:** A viral infection causing a painful rash, usually appearing as a single stripe of blisters wrapping around one side of the torso.
- **Priority Facts:** Caused by the reactivation of the varicella-zoster virus;

more common in older adults and individuals with weakened immune systems.
- **NCLEX Pearls:** Recognize early signs and symptoms for prompt treatment to reduce complications.
- **Top Safety Tips:** Isolate affected patients from those who have not had chickenpox, especially immunocompromised individuals.
- **Sample Question:** Which symptom is characteristically associated with Herpes Zoster (Shingles)? A. A widespread rash across both legs. B. A single stripe of painful blisters on one side of the body. C. Multiple cold sores around the mouth. D. A butterfly-shaped rash on the face.
- **Correct Answer:** B. A single stripe of painful blisters on one side of the body.
- **Rationale:** Herpes Zoster typically presents as a painful rash in a single stripe pattern on one side of the body, following a dermatome. The other options describe symptoms not typical of shingles.

Fungal Infections (e.g., Athlete's Foot)

- **Description:** Infections of the skin, hair, or nails caused by fungi, such as tinea pedis (athlete's foot).
- **Priority Facts:** Spread through direct contact with infected persons or surfaces; thrive in warm, moist environments.
- **NCLEX Pearls:** Emphasize prevention through hygiene and keeping affected areas dry and clean.
- **Top Safety Tips:** Advise patients to wear footwear in communal areas, avoid sharing personal items, and maintain good foot hygiene.
- **Sample Question:** The primary nursing intervention for preventing athlete's foot (tinea pedis) is: A. Prescribing oral antifungal medications. B. Recommending the use of occlusive footwear. C. Advising patients to keep feet dry and clean. D. Applying topical steroids to the affected area.
- **Correct Answer:** C. Advising patients to keep feet dry and clean.
- **Rationale:** The best prevention for athlete's foot is maintaining dry and clean feet to inhibit fungal growth. Oral antifungals and topical steroids

may be used for treatment, but are not primary preventive measures. Occlusive footwear should be avoided as it can create a moist environment conducive to fungal growth.

Vitiligo

- **Description:** A long-term skin condition characterized by patches of skin losing their pigment.
- **Priority Facts:** The cause is not fully understood but is believed to involve autoimmune destruction of melanocytes.
- **NCLEX Pearls:** Focus on psychological impacts, as the condition is more cosmetic than physically harmful.
- **Top Safety Tips:** Encourage the use of sunscreens and skin protection due to increased risk of sunburn in depigmented areas.
- **Sample Question:** A nurse is providing education to a patient with vitiligo. Which statement by the patient indicates a need for further teaching? A. "I should use sunscreen to protect my depigmented patches." B. "Vitiligo is highly contagious and I should avoid skin contact." C. "Wearing protective clothing can help prevent sunburn." D. "It's important to regularly examine my skin for any changes."
- **Correct Answer:** B. "Vitiligo is highly contagious and I should avoid skin contact."
- **Rationale:** Vitiligo is not contagious, and this misconception should be corrected. The use of sunscreen and protective clothing is important to protect depigmented areas from sunburn, and regular skin examinations are recommended.

Urticaria (Hives)

- **Description:** An outbreak of swollen, pale red bumps or plaques on the skin, often caused by an allergic reaction.
- **Priority Facts:** Can be triggered by allergens, medications, foods, or stress.

- **NCLEX Pearls:** Recognize and remove potential triggers, provide symptomatic relief.
- **Top Safety Tips:** Educate patients about identifying allergens and avoiding known triggers.
- **Sample Question:** The nurse recognizes that the FIRST line of treatment for acute urticaria (hives) is: A. Oral corticosteroids. B. Intravenous antibiotics. C. Antihistamines. D. Immunosuppressive therapy.
- **Correct Answer:** C. Antihistamines.
- **Rationale:** The first-line treatment for hives is antihistamines, which help alleviate itching and swelling. Corticosteroids may be used for severe cases, but are not the first choice. Antibiotics are not indicated unless there is a secondary infection, and immunosuppressive therapy is not a standard treatment for acute urticaria.

Hematologic System Disorders

Anemia (e.g., Iron Deficiency Anemia)

- **Description**: A condition in which there is a deficiency of red blood cells or hemoglobin, leading to fatigue, weakness, and shortness of breath.
- **Priority Facts**: Iron deficiency anemia is the most common type, often due to blood loss or a diet lacking in iron.
- **NCLEX Pearls**: Treatment includes iron supplementation and dietary changes.
- **Top Safety Tips**: Monitor for signs of fatigue and dizziness to prevent falls, and educate about iron-rich foods.
- **Sample Question**: What is a key nursing intervention for a patient with iron deficiency anemia?
- A. Encouraging high calcium intake with meals.
- B. Administering iron supplements with orange juice.
- C. Restricting fluid intake to concentrate iron levels.

- D. Providing a diet high in fatty foods.
- **Correct Answer**: B. Administering iron supplements with orange juice.
- **Rationale**: Vitamin C in orange juice enhances iron absorption, making it more effective when taken with iron supplements.

Hemophilia

- **Description**: A genetic disorder where blood doesn't clot normally, leading to excessive bleeding.
- **Priority Facts**: Can cause prolonged bleeding after injury, easy bruising, and joint damage.
- **NCLEX Pearls**: Treatment involves replacing the missing blood clotting factors.
- **Top Safety Tips**: Prevent injuries and manage bleeding episodes promptly.
- **Sample Question**: What is an essential aspect of care for a patient with hemophilia?
- A. Regular aspirin use for pain management.
- B. Applying firm pressure and ice to areas of bleeding.
- C. Encouraging participation in contact sports.
- D. Administering intramuscular injections frequently.
- **Correct Answer**: B. Applying firm pressure and ice to areas of bleeding.
- **Rationale**: Applying pressure and ice can help control and minimize bleeding episodes in hemophilia.

Leukemia

- **Description**: A type of cancer of the body's blood-forming tissues, including the bone marrow and the lymphatic system.
- **Priority Facts**: Characterized by the excessive production of abnormal white blood cells.
- **NCLEX Pearls**: Treatment includes chemotherapy, radiation therapy, and sometimes stem cell transplant.

- **Top Safety Tips**: Monitor for signs of infection and bleeding, and manage side effects of treatments.
- **Sample Question**: What is a priority nursing intervention for a patient undergoing treatment for leukemia?
- A. Isolating the patient in a sterile environment at all times.
- B. Encouraging high-intensity exercise to boost energy levels.
- C. Monitoring for and managing potential complications, like infection and anemia.
- D. Administering blood thinners routinely as a preventive measure.
- **Correct Answer**: C. Monitoring for and managing potential complications, like infection and anemia.
- **Rationale**: Patients with leukemia are at high risk for complications such as infection and anemia due to compromised immune function and treatment side effects.

Lymphoma

- **Description**: Cancer that originates in the lymphatic system, the disease-fighting network spread throughout the body.
- **Priority Facts**: There are two main types: Hodgkin lymphoma and non-Hodgkin lymphoma.
- **NCLEX Pearls**: Treatment may involve chemotherapy, radiation therapy, and immunotherapy.
- **Top Safety Tips**: Monitor for lymphedema and signs of infection, and provide supportive care during treatment.
- **Sample Question**: In caring for a patient with lymphoma, what is an important nursing consideration?
- A. Limiting all physical activities to reduce fatigue.
- B. Using heat application to swollen lymph nodes.
- C. Regularly assessing for and managing treatment side effects.
- D. Encouraging a high-sugar diet for energy.
- **Correct Answer**: C. Regularly assessing for and managing treatment side effects.

- **Rationale**: Managing the side effects of treatments like chemotherapy is critical for the well-being of lymphoma patients.

Deep Vein Thrombosis (DVT)

- **Description**: A blood clot that forms in a deep vein, usually in the legs, which can become life-threatening if the clot breaks loose and travels to the lungs.
- **Priority Facts**: Risk factors include prolonged immobility, surgery, and certain medical conditions.
- **NCLEX Pearls**: Prevention includes early ambulation, leg exercises, and anticoagulant therapy.
- **Top Safety Tips**: Educate about signs of DVT, such as leg swelling and pain, and monitor for signs of a pulmonary embolism.
- **Sample Question**: What is the MOST effective preventative measure for DVT in postoperative patients?
- A. Prolonged bed rest to promote healing.
- B. Application of heat to the lower extremities.
- C. Administration of prescribed anticoagulants.
- D. Frequent lower leg massages to improve circulation.
- **Correct Answer**: C. Administration of prescribed anticoagulants.
- **Rationale**: Anticoagulants are effective in preventing the formation of clots in patients at risk for DVT, especially after surgery.

Sickle Cell Disease

- **Description**: A genetic blood disorder characterized by red blood cells that assume an abnormal, rigid, sickle shape, leading to various complications.
- **Priority Facts**: Common in individuals of African descent. Symptoms include anemia, pain crises, and increased risk of infection.
- **NCLEX Pearls**: Management focuses on preventing crises, relieving symptoms, and preventing complications.

- **Top Safety Tips**: Monitor for signs of infection, manage pain effectively, and encourage hydration.
- **Sample Question**: What is a key nursing intervention for a patient experiencing a sickle cell crisis?
- A. Restrict fluids to reduce blood volume.
- B. Encourage ambulation to promote circulation.
- C. Administer oxygen and pain relief as prescribed.
- D. Apply cold packs to painful areas to reduce inflammation.
- **Correct Answer**: C. Administer oxygen and pain relief as prescribed.
- **Rationale**: Oxygen therapy and pain management are crucial during a sickle cell crisis to improve oxygen delivery and alleviate pain.

Thrombocytopenia

- **Description**: A condition characterized by abnormally low levels of platelets, leading to increased bleeding and bruising.
- **Priority Facts**: Can result from various conditions, including leukemia, certain medications, and autoimmune diseases.
- **NCLEX Pearls**: Treatment depends on the cause and may include blood transfusions or steroids.
- **Top Safety Tips**: Monitor for signs of bleeding, use soft-bristle toothbrushes, and avoid invasive procedures.
- **Sample Question**: What is a priority nursing action for a patient with thrombocytopenia?
- A. Encouraging the use of over-the-counter pain relievers like aspirin.
- B. Implementing fall precautions and monitoring for signs of bleeding.
- C. Restricting physical activity to bed rest.
- D. Administering platelet transfusions daily.
- **Correct Answer**: B. Implementing fall precautions and monitoring for signs of bleeding.
- **Rationale**: Patients with thrombocytopenia are at increased risk of bleeding; hence, minimizing injury risk and monitoring for bleeding is essential.

Hemochromatosis

- **Description**: An inherited disorder where the body absorbs too much iron from the diet, leading to iron overload.
- **Priority Facts**: Excess iron can deposit in organs, particularly the liver, heart, and pancreas, leading to organ damage.
- **NCLEX Pearls**: Treatment includes phlebotomy (blood removal) and chelation therapy.
- **Top Safety Tips**: Educate about low-iron diets and monitor liver function.
- **Sample Question**: What dietary advice is MOST appropriate for a patient with hemochromatosis?
- A. Increase consumption of red meat and iron-rich foods.
- B. Consume a high-calcium diet to enhance iron absorption.
- C. Avoid supplements containing iron and vitamin C.
- D. High fiber diet to promote iron excretion.
- **Correct Answer**: C. Avoid supplements containing iron and vitamin C.
- **Rationale**: Iron and vitamin C supplements can exacerbate iron overload in hemochromatosis patients.

Myelodysplastic Syndromes

- **Description**: A group of disorders caused by poorly formed or dysfunctional blood cells, often progressing to anemia or leukemia.
- **Priority Facts**: Symptoms include fatigue, shortness of breath, and easy bruising or bleeding.
- **NCLEX Pearls**: Treatment may include blood transfusions, medication, or bone marrow transplant.
- **Top Safety Tips**: Monitor for and manage symptoms of anemia and infection.
- **Sample Question**: What is an important consideration in the care of a patient with myelodysplastic syndromes?
- A. Routine administration of high-dose chemotherapy.
- B. Regular blood transfusions to manage anemia.

- C. Increasing physical exercise to stimulate bone marrow function.
- D. Strict dietary restrictions to improve blood cell production.
- **Correct Answer**: B. Regular blood transfusions to manage anemia.
- **Rationale**: Blood transfusions are often necessary in myelodysplastic syndromes to manage anemia due to insufficient red blood cell production.

Multiple Myeloma

- **Description**: A type of cancer that forms in plasma cells, causing cancer cells to accumulate in the bone marrow and interfere with the production of normal blood cells.
- **Priority Facts**: Symptoms include bone pain, anemia, kidney dysfunction, and increased risk of infections.
- **NCLEX Pearls**: Treatment includes chemotherapy, targeted therapy, and sometimes stem cell transplant.
- **Top Safety Tips**: Monitor for bone fractures, kidney function, and signs of infection.
- **Sample Question**: What is a key nursing intervention for a patient with multiple myeloma?
- A. Encouraging weight-bearing exercises to strengthen bones.
- B. Applying heat to areas of bone pain.
- C. Monitoring for and managing symptoms such as bone pain and fatigue.
- D. Restricting fluids to prevent fluid overload.
- **Correct Answer**: C. Monitoring for and managing symptoms such as bone pain and fatigue.
- **Rationale**: Symptom management, including pain and fatigue, is crucial in the care of patients with multiple myeloma due to bone involvement and anemia.

Immune System Disorders

Rheumatoid Arthritis

- **Description**: A chronic inflammatory disorder affecting joints, including those in the hands and feet.
- **Priority Facts**: It's an autoimmune disorder that causes joint inflammation and pain.
- **NCLEX Pearls**: Treatment includes disease-modifying antirheumatic drugs (DMARDs) and physical therapy.
- **Top Safety Tips**: Monitor for medication side effects and encourage joint-protective techniques.
- **Sample Question**: What is an essential strategy in the care of a patient with rheumatoid arthritis?
- A. Maintaining strict bed rest during flare-ups.
- B. Encouraging regular, gentle exercise to maintain joint function.
- C. Using high-impact exercises to strengthen affected joints.
- D. Avoiding all medications to prevent side effects.
- **Correct Answer**: B. Encouraging regular, gentle exercise to maintain joint function.
- **Rationale**: Regular, gentle exercises help maintain flexibility and strength without causing additional joint damage in rheumatoid arthritis patients.

Systemic Lupus Erythematosus (SLE)

- **Description**: An autoimmune disease that can affect various body systems, including joints, skin, kidneys, blood cells, brain, heart, and lungs.
- **Priority Facts**: Characterized by periods of illness (flares) and remissions.
- **NCLEX Pearls**: Management includes corticosteroids, immunosuppressants, and lifestyle modifications.
- **Top Safety Tips**: Educate about sun protection and monitoring for signs of organ involvement.
- **Sample Question**: What is important to include in patient education for

systemic lupus erythematosus?
- A. Avoiding all physical activity to prevent fatigue.
- B. Using sunscreen and protective clothing when outdoors.
- C. Discontinuing medications during symptom remission.
- D. Increasing salt intake to manage kidney involvement.
- **Correct Answer**: B. Using sunscreen and protective clothing when outdoors.
- **Rationale**: Sun exposure can exacerbate SLE symptoms, so protection from UV rays is essential.

Inflammatory Bowel Disease (IBD) - Crohn's & Ulcerative Colitis

- **Description**: Chronic conditions that cause inflammation of the gastrointestinal tract. Crohn's can affect any part of the GI tract, while ulcerative colitis is limited to the colon and rectum.
- **Priority Facts**: Symptoms include diarrhea, abdominal pain, weight loss, and fatigue.
- **NCLEX Pearls**: Treatment involves anti-inflammatory drugs, immune system suppressors, and sometimes surgery.
- **Top Safety Tips**: Monitor nutritional status and educate about dietary management.
- **Sample Question**: What dietary recommendation is generally advised for patients with IBD?
- A. High-fiber diet to promote bowel regularity.
- B. Low-residue diet during flare-ups to reduce bowel irritation.
- C. High-fat diet for increased calorie intake.
- D. Unrestricted dairy products to enhance calcium intake.
- **Correct Answer**: B. Low-residue diet during flare-ups to reduce bowel irritation.
- **Rationale**: A low-residue diet can help reduce the frequency of bowel movements and abdominal pain during IBD flare-ups.

Type 1 Diabetes Mellitus

- **Description**: An autoimmune condition where the pancreas produces little or no insulin.
- **Priority Facts**: Requires life-long insulin therapy and close blood sugar monitoring.
- **NCLEX Pearls**: Educate about insulin administration, carbohydrate counting, and hypoglycemia management.
- **Top Safety Tips**: Monitor blood glucose levels regularly and recognize signs of hypo- and hyperglycemia.
- **Sample Question**: What is a crucial aspect of management for a patient with Type 1 diabetes mellitus?
- A. Avoiding all physical activity to prevent hypoglycemia.
- B. Administering oral hypoglycemic agents.
- C. Monitoring blood glucose levels and administering insulin as prescribed.
- D. Implementing a low-protein diet to preserve kidney function.
- **Correct Answer**: C. Monitoring blood glucose levels and administering insulin as prescribed.
- **Rationale**: Continuous monitoring of blood glucose and proper insulin administration are vital for managing Type 1 diabetes.

Multiple Sclerosis

- **Description**: A chronic disease of the central nervous system marked by damage to the myelin sheath that covers nerve fibers.
- **Priority Facts**: Symptoms can include muscle weakness, coordination problems, and cognitive changes.
- **NCLEX Pearls**: Management includes disease-modifying therapies, symptom management, and rehabilitation strategies.
- **Top Safety Tips**: Assist with mobility, prevent falls, and monitor for cognitive changes.
- **Sample Question**: What is an important nursing intervention for a

patient with multiple sclerosis?
- A. Encouraging complete bed rest during exacerbations.
- B. Implementing passive range-of-motion exercises to maintain mobility.
- C. Recommending a high-carbohydrate diet for energy.
- D. Avoiding all social interactions to reduce stress.
- **Correct Answer**: B. Implementing passive range-of-motion exercises to maintain mobility.
- **Rationale**: Regular range-of-motion exercises can help maintain muscle function and flexibility in patients with multiple sclerosis.

Psoriasis

- **Description**: A chronic autoimmune condition that accelerates the life cycle of skin cells, causing red, scaly patches that are often itchy or painful.
- **Priority Facts**: Can be associated with other serious health conditions, such as heart disease and diabetes.
- **NCLEX Pearls**: Management includes topical treatments, phototherapy, and systemic medications.
- **Top Safety Tips**: Educate about skin care, trigger avoidance, and adherence to treatment regimens.
- **Sample Question**: What is an important self-care measure for a patient with psoriasis?
- A. Frequent sunbathing without sunscreen.
- B. Using moisturizers to reduce skin dryness.
- C. Scrubbing skin lesions vigorously.
- D. Applying high-dose topical corticosteroids continuously.
- **Correct Answer**: B. Using moisturizers to reduce skin dryness.
- **Rationale**: Moisturizing helps to reduce the dryness, itching, and scaling associated with psoriasis.

Guillain-Barré Syndrome

- **Description**: A rare disorder in which the body's immune system attacks the nerves, leading to muscle weakness and sometimes paralysis.
- **Priority Facts**: The exact cause is unknown, but it often follows an infectious illness.
- **NCLEX Pearls**: Treatment includes plasma exchange and intravenous immunoglobulins.
- **Top Safety Tips**: Monitor respiratory function and provide supportive care during recovery.
- **Sample Question**: What is the priority nursing intervention for a patient diagnosed with Guillain-Barré Syndrome?
- A. Encouraging intense exercise to regain muscle strength.
- B. Administering antibiotics as a preventive measure.
- C. Monitoring respiratory status and providing ventilatory support if needed.
- D. Implementing a high-protein diet to speed up nerve repair.
- **Correct Answer**: C. Monitoring respiratory status and providing ventilatory support if needed.
- **Rationale**: Guillain-Barré Syndrome can progress rapidly, potentially leading to respiratory failure, so close monitoring of respiratory function is critical.

Graves' Disease

- **Description**: An autoimmune disorder that results in the overproduction of thyroid hormones (hyperthyroidism).
- **Priority Facts**: Symptoms include anxiety, hand tremor, heat sensitivity, weight loss, and bulging eyes.
- **NCLEX Pearls**: Treatment includes radioactive iodine, medications, and sometimes surgery.
- **Top Safety Tips**: Monitor heart rate and rhythm, educate about medication adherence, and watch for signs of thyrotoxic crisis.

- **Sample Question**: What is a key aspect of managing care for a patient with Graves' Disease?
- A. Restricting all iodine intake.
- B. Increasing caloric intake to counteract weight loss.
- C. Administering sedatives routinely to manage anxiety.
- D. Monitoring for signs of hyperthyroidism and advising regular follow-ups.
- **Correct Answer**: D. Monitoring for signs of hyperthyroidism and advising regular follow-ups.
- **Rationale**: Regular monitoring is important to manage the symptoms of hyperthyroidism and adjust treatment as needed.

Celiac Disease

- **Description**: An autoimmune disorder where ingestion of gluten leads to damage in the small intestine.
- **Priority Facts**: Can cause symptoms like diarrhea, bloating, and weight loss, and if untreated, can lead to serious complications.
- **NCLEX Pearls**: Strict adherence to a gluten-free diet is the only effective treatment.
- **Top Safety Tips**: Educate about gluten-containing foods and cross-contamination.
- **Sample Question**: What dietary modification is MOST essential for a patient diagnosed with celiac disease?
- A. Low-fat diet.
- B. High-protein diet.
- C. Gluten-free diet.
- D. Lactose-free diet.
- **Correct Answer**: C. Gluten-free diet.
- **Rationale**: Avoiding gluten is essential in celiac disease to prevent immune reaction and intestinal damage.

Allergic Reactions (e.g., Hay Fever, Asthma, Anaphylaxis)

- **Description**: An allergic reaction is an immune response to a foreign substance that's not typically harmful to the body. These foreign substances are called allergens.
- **Priority Facts**: Allergic reactions can range from mild, like hay fever, to severe, like anaphylaxis.
- **NCLEX Pearls**: Treatment varies from antihistamines for mild reactions to epinephrine for anaphylaxis.
- **Top Safety Tips**: Educate about avoiding known allergens and carrying emergency medication (like epinephrine auto-injectors).
- **Sample Question**: What is the MOST important action for a nurse when a patient is experiencing anaphylaxis?
- A. Waiting for symptoms to resolve on their own.
- B. Immediately administering an oral antihistamine.
- C. Administering epinephrine as soon as possible.
- D. Placing the patient in a supine position and elevating the legs.
- **Correct Answer**: C. Administering epinephrine as soon as possible.
- **Rationale**: Immediate administration of epinephrine is crucial in anaphylaxis to counteract severe allergic reactions and prevent shock.

Oncological Disorders

Breast Cancer

- **Description**: A type of cancer that develops from breast tissue, characterized by a lump in the breast or changes in breast shape or texture.
- **Priority Facts**: Risk factors include age, family history, and certain genetic mutations.
- **NCLEX Pearls**: Treatment may involve surgery, chemotherapy, radiation therapy, and hormonal therapy.
- **Top Safety Tips**: Educate about self-examination, mammography, and adherence to treatment plans.

- **Sample Question**: What is a crucial aspect of postoperative care for a patient who has undergone a mastectomy?
- A. Encouraging upper body exercises immediately after surgery.
- B. Monitoring for lymphedema and providing arm care on the affected side.
- C. Applying heat to the surgical site to promote healing.
- D. Restricting all arm movement on the side of the surgery.
- **Correct Answer**: B. Monitoring for lymphedema and providing arm care on the affected side.
- **Rationale**: Post-mastectomy care includes monitoring for lymphedema and educating about exercises to maintain arm function and prevent swelling.

Lung Cancer

- **Description**: A type of cancer that originates in the lungs, often associated with smoking and exposure to radon gas.
- **Priority Facts**: Symptoms include a persistent cough, chest pain, and shortness of breath.
- **NCLEX Pearls**: Treatment may include surgery, chemotherapy, and radiation therapy.
- **Top Safety Tips**: Monitor respiratory status and educate about smoking cessation and radon exposure.
- **Sample Question**: What is an important nursing intervention for a patient undergoing treatment for lung cancer?
- A. Encouraging bed rest and limited activity.
- B. Administering oxygen at high flow rates.
- C. Monitoring for side effects of treatment and managing symptoms.
- D. Recommending smoking to stimulate lung function.
- **Correct Answer**: C. Monitoring for side effects of treatment and managing symptoms.
- **Rationale**: Monitoring and managing the side effects of cancer treatment, such as nausea, fatigue, and respiratory issues, are crucial in lung cancer

care.

Prostate Cancer

- **Description**: A form of cancer that develops in the prostate gland, usually occurring in older men.
- **Priority Facts**: Often presents with difficulty in urination, blood in urine, or erectile dysfunction.
- **NCLEX Pearls**: Treatment options include surgery, radiation therapy, hormone therapy, and chemotherapy.
- **Top Safety Tips**: Educate about regular prostate screenings and managing side effects of treatment.
- **Sample Question**: What is a key aspect of care for a patient with prostate cancer undergoing hormone therapy?
- A. Increasing calcium and vitamin D intake to prevent osteoporosis.
- B. Regular intake of aspirin to prevent blood clots.
- C. Encouraging high-fat diet for weight gain.
- D. Limiting fluid intake to reduce urinary frequency.
- **Correct Answer**: A. Increasing calcium and vitamin D intake to prevent osteoporosis.
- **Rationale**: Hormone therapy can weaken bones; therefore, increasing calcium and vitamin D is important to prevent osteoporosis.

Colorectal Cancer

- **Description**: Cancer that starts in the colon or rectum, part of the digestive tract.
- **Priority Facts**: Symptoms include changes in bowel habits, blood in stool, and abdominal discomfort.
- **NCLEX Pearls**: Treatment often involves surgery, chemotherapy, and radiation therapy.
- **Top Safety Tips**: Educate about colonoscopy screening and dietary factors.

- **Sample Question**: What is the MOST effective way to prevent colorectal cancer in at-risk populations?
- A. Regular colorectal screening starting at an appropriate age.
- B. Taking antibiotics as a preventive measure.
- C. Using laxatives regularly to cleanse the colon.
- D. Adopting a strictly vegetarian diet.
- **Correct Answer**: A. Regular colorectal screening starting at an appropriate age.
- **Rationale**: Regular screening, such as colonoscopy, is crucial for early detection and prevention of colorectal cancer.

Leukemia

- **Description**: A type of cancer of the body's blood-forming tissues, including the bone marrow and the lymphatic system.
- **Priority Facts**: Characterized by the excessive production of abnormal white blood cells.
- **NCLEX Pearls**: Treatment includes chemotherapy, targeted therapy, radiation therapy, and stem cell transplant.
- **Top Safety Tips**: Monitor for signs of infection, anemia, and bleeding.
- **Sample Question**: What is a priority nursing intervention for a patient undergoing chemotherapy for leukemia?
- A. Implementing strict isolation to prevent all physical contact.
- B. Administering aspirin for pain or fever.
- C. Monitoring for and managing potential complications, like infection and anemia.
- D. Encouraging high-intensity physical activity to build strength.
- **Correct Answer**: C. Monitoring for and managing potential complications, like infection and anemia.
- **Rationale**: Patients with leukemia are particularly susceptible to infections and anemia due to the effects of the disease and chemotherapy on the immune system and blood cells.

Lymphoma

- **Description**: A type of cancer that originates in the lymphatic system, which is part of the immune system.
- **Priority Facts**: Includes two main types: Hodgkin's lymphoma and non-Hodgkin's lymphoma.
- **NCLEX Pearls**: Treatment varies based on type and stage and may include chemotherapy, radiation therapy, and stem cell transplant.
- **Top Safety Tips**: Monitor for lymphedema, signs of infection, and manage side effects of chemotherapy.
- **Sample Question**: What nursing action is important for a patient receiving chemotherapy for lymphoma?
- A. Avoiding all physical activity.
- B. Administering aspirin for fever.
- C. Monitoring for infection and managing nausea.
- D. Applying heat to swollen lymph nodes.
- **Correct Answer**: C. Monitoring for infection and managing nausea.
- **Rationale**: Chemotherapy can lower immunity, increasing infection risk. Managing side effects like nausea is also crucial for patient comfort.

Skin Cancer (Melanoma)

- **Description**: A serious form of skin cancer that begins in cells known as melanocytes.
- **Priority Facts**: Risk factors include excessive sun exposure and a history of sunburns.
- **NCLEX Pearls**: Early detection through skin exams is crucial. The ABCDE rule (Asymmetry, Border, Color, Diameter, Evolving) helps identify problematic moles.
- **Top Safety Tips**: Educate about sun protection and regular skin self-examinations.
- **Sample Question**: What is the MOST effective preventative measure against melanoma?

- A. Regular tanning bed use to build a base tan.
- B. Applying sunscreen with an SPF of 30 or higher.
- C. Using high-dose vitamin D supplements.
- D. Exfoliating skin regularly to remove dead cells.
- **Correct Answer**: B. Applying sunscreen with an SPF of 30 or higher.
- **Rationale**: Using sunscreen helps protect the skin from harmful UV rays, significantly reducing the risk of melanoma.

Pancreatic Cancer

- **Description**: A type of cancer that begins in the pancreas, an organ behind the lower part of the stomach.
- **Priority Facts**: Symptoms often don't appear until the disease is advanced and may include abdominal pain, weight loss, and jaundice.
- **NCLEX Pearls**: Treatment options may include surgery, chemotherapy, and radiation therapy.
- **Top Safety Tips**: Manage pain effectively and monitor for digestive issues.
- **Sample Question**: What is a key nursing intervention for a patient with advanced pancreatic cancer?
- A. Restricting all oral food and fluids.
- B. Encouraging high-impact exercise.
- C. Administering pain medication and providing nutritional support.
- D. Performing frequent high-intensity abdominal exercises.
- **Correct Answer**: C. Administering pain medication and providing nutritional support.
- **Rationale**: Pain management and nutritional support are critical in managing pancreatic cancer due to symptoms like abdominal pain and weight loss.

Ovarian Cancer

- **Description**: A type of cancer that begins in the ovaries.
- **Priority Facts**: Often detected late due to vague symptoms like bloating, pelvic pain, and abdominal swelling.
- **NCLEX Pearls**: Treatment typically includes surgery and chemotherapy.
- **Top Safety Tips**: Monitor for abdominal discomfort and changes in bowel habits.
- **Sample Question**: What is important for early detection of ovarian cancer?
- A. Annual Pap smears.
- B. Regular pelvic examinations and awareness of symptoms.
- C. Frequent high-dose estrogen therapy.
- D. Routine ultrasound every six months.
- **Correct Answer**: B. Regular pelvic examinations and awareness of symptoms.
- **Rationale**: Regular pelvic exams and being aware of the symptoms can aid in earlier detection of ovarian cancer.

Bladder Cancer

- **Description**: A type of cancer that occurs in the bladder, the organ that stores urine.
- **Priority Facts**: Common symptoms include blood in urine, frequent urination, and pain during urination.
- **NCLEX Pearls**: Treatment may include surgery, intravesical therapy, chemotherapy, and radiation therapy.
- **Top Safety Tips**: Educate about smoking cessation and monitor for urinary symptoms.
- **Sample Question**: What is an essential aspect of care for a patient undergoing treatment for bladder cancer?
- A. Limiting fluid intake to reduce urinary frequency.
- B. Regular cystoscopies to monitor for recurrence.

- C. Using urinary catheters long-term to manage incontinence.
- D. Applying heat to the abdominal area to relieve pain.
- **Correct Answer**: B. Regular cystoscopies to monitor for recurrence.
- **Rationale**: Regular cystoscopies are important for detecting bladder cancer recurrence and monitoring the effectiveness of treatment.

3

Adult Medical-Surgical Nursing Part 2

Perioperative Nursing Care

- **Description**: Nursing care provided before, during, and after surgery.
- **Priority Facts**: Involves preoperative assessment, intraoperative management, and postoperative recovery.
- **NCLEX Pearls**: Focus on patient education, surgical site infection prevention, and pain management.
- **Top Safety Tips**: Monitor vital signs, wound condition, and pain levels; prevent deep vein thrombosis (DVT) and pulmonary complications.
- **Sample Question**: What is a critical action by the nurse in the immediate postoperative period?
- A. Encouraging the patient to drink fluids to avoid dehydration.
- B. Monitoring respiratory status and managing pain.
- C. Ambulating the patient immediately after surgery to prevent DVT.
- D. Administering a sedative to promote sleep.
- **Correct Answer**: B. Monitoring respiratory status and managing pain.
- **Rationale**: Postoperative care involves close monitoring of the patient's respiratory status to prevent complications and managing pain for comfort and recovery.

Chronic Disease Management

- **Description**: Ongoing care and support for patients with chronic illnesses to improve their health and quality of life.
- **Priority Facts**: Includes managing symptoms, medication adherence, and lifestyle modifications.
- **NCLEX Pearls**: Focus on patient education, regular monitoring, and coordination of care.
- **Top Safety Tips**: Educate about disease process, medication side effects, and when to seek medical help.
- **Sample Question**: What is essential for effective chronic disease management in patients with diabetes?
- A. Limiting carbohydrate intake to an extreme level.
- B. Regular blood glucose monitoring and medication adherence.
- C. Using alternative herbal medicines in place of prescribed medications.
- D. Engaging in high-intensity exercise regardless of fitness level.
- **Correct Answer**: B. Regular blood glucose monitoring and medication adherence.
- **Rationale**: For chronic conditions like diabetes, consistent monitoring of blood glucose and adherence to prescribed medication regimens are key to managing the disease effectively.

Pain Management in Medical-Surgical Patients

- **Description**: The process of providing relief to patients experiencing acute or chronic pain due to medical or surgical conditions.
- **Priority Facts**: Pain can be managed through pharmacological means (medication) and non-pharmacological methods (like physical therapy, relaxation techniques).
- **NCLEX Pearls**: Assess pain regularly and tailor pain management strategies to individual patient needs.
- **Top Safety Tips**: Monitor for medication side effects and the effectiveness of pain relief methods.

- **Sample Question**: What is a critical consideration in managing pain for a postoperative patient?
- A. Administering pain medication only when the pain is severe.
- B. Regularly assessing pain levels and administering prescribed analgesics.
- C. Relying solely on patient self-report for pain assessment.
- D. Using only non-pharmacological methods for pain control.
- **Correct Answer**: B. Regularly assessing pain levels and administering prescribed analgesics.
- **Rationale**: Regular assessment of pain and timely administration of analgesics are crucial in effectively managing postoperative pain.

Nutritional Management in Medical-Surgical Conditions

- **Description**: Dietary planning and monitoring to support the treatment and recovery of patients with various medical-surgical conditions.
- **Priority Facts**: Nutritional needs vary based on the specific condition and patient factors.
- **NCLEX Pearls**: Assess nutritional status, provide diet education, and coordinate with dietitians for specialized diets.
- **Top Safety Tips**: Monitor for signs of malnutrition or dehydration and educate about appropriate dietary modifications.
- **Sample Question**: What is important in nutritional management for a patient with heart failure?
- A. Encouraging a high-sodium diet to increase fluid retention.
- B. Implementing a low-sodium diet to reduce fluid overload.
- C. Promoting an unrestricted fluid intake.
- D. Focusing solely on calorie intake without regard to nutrient quality.
- **Correct Answer**: B. Implementing a low-sodium diet to reduce fluid overload.
- **Rationale**: A low-sodium diet is essential in heart failure management to prevent fluid retention and reduce the burden on the heart.

Wound Care and Pressure Injury Management

- **Description**: Techniques and practices to promote the healing of wounds and prevent or treat pressure injuries.
- **Priority Facts**: Includes regular wound assessment, appropriate dressing, and pressure relief strategies.
- **NCLEX Pearls**: Focus on maintaining a clean wound environment, monitoring for signs of infection, and repositioning immobile patients.
- **Top Safety Tips**: Educate about the importance of wound cleanliness, adherence to treatment, and mobility.
- **Sample Question**: What is a key nursing action in the prevention of pressure injuries in bedridden patients?
- A. Keeping the patient in one position to avoid disturbing the wound.
- B. Massaging over bony prominences to improve circulation.
- C. Regular repositioning and use of pressure-relieving devices.
- D. Applying heat pads to relieve pressure areas.
- **Correct Answer**: C. Regular repositioning and use of pressure-relieving devices.
- **Rationale**: Regularly repositioning patients and using devices like specialized mattresses help distribute pressure and prevent injury to the skin.

Infectious Diseases and Isolation Precautions

- **Description**: Management of diseases caused by bacteria, viruses, fungi, or parasites, often requiring specific isolation precautions to prevent spread.
- **Priority Facts**: Includes diseases like MRSA, tuberculosis, and COVID-19.
- **NCLEX Pearls**: Use appropriate personal protective equipment (PPE) and follow CDC guidelines for each type of isolation precaution.
- **Top Safety Tips**: Educate staff and visitors about proper hand hygiene and PPE use.
- **Sample Question**: What is essential when caring for a patient with

airborne precautions?
- A. Using a standard surgical mask at all times in the room.
- B. Wearing an N95 respirator when in the patient's room.
- C. Limiting use of gloves to only direct patient contact.
- D. Allowing unrestricted visitation to promote social interaction.
- **Correct Answer**: B. Wearing an N95 respirator when in the patient's room.
- **Rationale**: An N95 respirator is required for airborne precautions to prevent inhalation of infectious agents (e.g., tuberculosis).

Transfusion Reactions and Blood Product Administration

- **Description**: The clinical process of administering blood products and managing potential adverse reactions.
- **Priority Facts**: Common reactions include febrile, allergic, and hemolytic reactions.
- **NCLEX Pearls**: Verify patient identity and blood product compatibility; monitor for signs of reaction.
- **Top Safety Tips**: Stay with the patient during the first 15-30 minutes of transfusion and monitor vital signs.
- **Sample Question**: What is the FIRST action by the nurse if a transfusion reaction is suspected?
- A. Slow the transfusion rate and monitor the patient.
- B. Stop the transfusion and maintain IV with saline solution.
- C. Administer antihistamines to control allergic response.
- D. Immediately start a new blood transfusion of a different type.
- **Correct Answer**: B. Stop the transfusion and maintain IV with saline solution.
- **Rationale**: Stopping the transfusion and maintaining an IV line with saline prevents further reaction while allowing for emergency medication administration if necessary.

Intravenous Therapy and Central Venous Access

- **Description**: Administration of fluids, medications, and nutrition directly into veins, often via central venous access for long-term use.
- **Priority Facts**: Central lines include PICC lines, central venous catheters, and port-a-caths.
- **NCLEX Pearls**: Ensure proper line placement, use aseptic technique, and monitor for complications like infection and thrombosis.
- **Top Safety Tips**: Regular assessment of insertion sites and adherence to infection control protocols.
- **Sample Question**: What is crucial in the maintenance of a central venous catheter?
- A. Flushing the line with saline or heparin as prescribed.
- B. Using the line for frequent blood draws only.
- C. Applying antibiotic ointment daily at the insertion site.
- D. Changing the catheter every three days as a standard practice.
- **Correct Answer**: A. Flushing the line with saline or heparin as prescribed.
- **Rationale**: Flushing a central venous catheter as prescribed is key to maintaining patency and preventing occlusion or infection.

Emergency and Trauma Nursing

- **Description**: Nursing care focused on the assessment, stabilization, and treatment of patients in emergency and acute trauma situations.
- **Priority Facts**: Rapid triage and treatment of life-threatening conditions are essential.
- **NCLEX Pearls**: Utilize the ABCDE (Airway, Breathing, Circulation, Disability, Exposure) approach in trauma assessment.
- **Top Safety Tips**: Prioritize life-saving interventions and always be prepared for sudden changes in patient condition.
- **Sample Question**: In a trauma patient, what is the nurse's FIRST priority?
- A. Establishing IV access.
- B. Assessing the patient's airway and breathing.

- C. Applying a cervical collar.
- D. Administering pain medication.
- **Correct Answer**: B. Assessing the patient's airway and breathing.
- **Rationale**: Ensuring a patent airway and adequate breathing is the first and most critical step in trauma care.

Shock: Types and Management

- **Description**: A life-threatening condition where the circulatory system fails to provide adequate tissue perfusion, leading to organ dysfunction.
- **Priority Facts**: Types of shock include hypovolemic, cardiogenic, distributive (e.g., septic, anaphylactic, neurogenic), and obstructive.
- **NCLEX Pearls**: Management varies by type but generally includes fluid resuscitation, vasopressors, and treating the underlying cause.
- **Top Safety Tips**: Monitor vital signs, urine output, and consciousness; provide oxygen and fluids as needed.
- **Sample Question**: What is the MOST appropriate initial intervention for a patient in hypovolemic shock?
- A. Immediate administration of high-dose corticosteroids.
- B. Rapid infusion of IV fluids to restore circulating volume.
- C. Placing the patient in a Trendelenburg position.
- D. Providing supplemental oxygen only if SpO2 is below 90%.
- **Correct Answer**: B. Rapid infusion of IV fluids to restore circulating volume.
- **Rationale**: In hypovolemic shock, the primary goal is to restore intravascular volume. Rapid infusion of IV fluids is essential for increasing blood volume and improving perfusion.

Sepsis and Septic Shock

- **Description**: Sepsis is a life-threatening response to infection that can lead to tissue damage, organ failure, and death. Septic shock is a severe and potentially fatal condition that occurs as a complication of sepsis.

- **Priority Facts**: Early recognition and treatment of sepsis are crucial for survival.
- **NCLEX Pearls**: Management includes broad-spectrum antibiotics, fluid resuscitation, and vasopressors if necessary.
- **Top Safety Tips**: Monitor vital signs, maintain aseptic technique, and educate about early signs of infection.
- **Sample Question**: What is the FIRST priority in the management of a patient with suspected sepsis?
- A. Administering high-dose corticosteroids.
- B. Immediate initiation of broad-spectrum antibiotics.
- C. Waiting for culture results before starting any treatment.
- D. Applying a heating pad to reduce chills.
- **Correct Answer**: B. Immediate initiation of broad-spectrum antibiotics.
- **Rationale**: Early administration of broad-spectrum antibiotics is critical in sepsis management to fight the underlying infection.

Burns: Assessment and Management

- **Description**: Burns are injuries to tissues caused by heat, radiation, electricity, or chemicals.
- **Priority Facts**: Severity is determined by burn depth, size, location, and patient age and health.
- **NCLEX Pearls**: Treatment involves fluid resuscitation, pain management, and wound care.
- **Top Safety Tips**: Assess for airway compromise, prevent infection, and manage pain.
- **Sample Question**: What is a key aspect of care for a patient with major burns?
- A. Limiting fluid intake to prevent edema.
- B. Administering large volumes of IV fluids based on burn severity.
- C. Using ice directly on burn areas to relieve pain.
- D. Encouraging high-intensity exercise to promote skin healing.
- **Correct Answer**: B. Administering large volumes of IV fluids based on

burn severity.
- **Rationale**: Fluid resuscitation is critical in major burns to prevent shock and organ failure due to fluid loss from the injury.

Poisoning and Overdose Management

- **Description**: Management of the ingestion, inhalation, or absorption of toxic substances.
- **Priority Facts**: Treatment varies depending on the substance involved and the severity of the symptoms.
- **NCLEX Pearls**: Key actions include stabilizing the patient, preventing further absorption, and administering antidotes when appropriate.
- **Top Safety Tips**: Monitor vital signs and neurological status, and prepare for potential complications.
- **Sample Question**: What is an immediate nursing action following the ingestion of a toxic substance?
- A. Inducing vomiting to expel the poison.
- B. Administering activated charcoal, if appropriate.
- C. Waiting for symptoms to develop before treatment.
- D. Giving large amounts of water to dilute the substance.
- **Correct Answer**: B. Administering activated charcoal, if appropriate.
- **Rationale**: Activated charcoal can bind to certain toxins in the gastrointestinal tract, preventing absorption.

Bioterrorism and Disaster Response in Nursing

- **Description**: Nursing care and management during bioterrorism events or disasters.
- **Priority Facts**: Involves emergency preparedness, rapid response, and effective coordination of resources.
- **NCLEX Pearls**: Recognize potential signs of bioterrorism, understand decontamination procedures, and know disaster response protocols.
- **Top Safety Tips**: Use appropriate PPE, maintain a high level of suspicion

in unusual presentations, and participate in disaster drills.
- **Sample Question**: What is an essential role of the nurse in a bioterrorism event?
- A. Waiting for official confirmation before reporting suspicious symptoms.
- B. Rapidly identifying and reporting unusual patterns of illness.
- C. Administering antibiotics to all patients as a preventive measure.
- D. Isolating all patients with respiratory symptoms immediately.
- **Correct Answer**: B. Rapidly identifying and reporting unusual patterns of illness.
- **Rationale**: Early detection and reporting of unusual illness patterns can be crucial in responding effectively to a bioterrorism event.

Palliative and End-of-Life Care in Medical-Surgical Settings

- **Description**: Care focused on providing relief from the symptoms and stress of serious illness, with a goal of improving quality of life.
- **Priority Facts**: Involves managing pain and other distressing symptoms, and providing psychological, social, and spiritual support.
- **NCLEX Pearls**: Communicate effectively with patients and families, and respect patient wishes regarding end-of-life care.
- **Top Safety Tips**: Ensure comfort, manage symptoms, and support the family during the process.
- **Sample Question**: What is a priority for providing palliative care to a terminally ill patient?
- A. Aggressively treating the disease.
- B. Focusing solely on physical symptoms.
- C. Providing comprehensive pain and symptom management.
- D. Encouraging the patient to participate in strenuous activities.
- **Correct Answer**: C. Providing comprehensive pain and symptom management.
- **Rationale**: In palliative care, the primary focus is on relieving pain and other distressing symptoms, enhancing the quality of life for the patient

and their family.

Patient Safety and Quality Improvement

- **Description**: A healthcare discipline focused on developing procedures, policies, and practices to enhance the safety and quality of patient care.
- **Priority Facts**: Involves identifying risk factors, preventing errors, and creating a culture of safety.
- **NCLEX Pearls**: Emphasize the importance of communication, teamwork, and continuous learning in improving patient outcomes.
- **Top Safety Tips**: Follow evidence-based practices, encourage reporting of errors or near misses, and implement corrective actions.
- **Sample Question**: What is a key component of quality improvement in healthcare settings?
- A. Decreasing the number of staff to patient ratio.
- B. Implementing evidence-based guidelines and protocols.
- C. Avoiding disclosure of errors to patients and families.
- D. Focusing solely on cost-cutting measures.
- **Correct Answer**: B. Implementing evidence-based guidelines and protocols.
- **Rationale**: Evidence-based guidelines and protocols are essential in improving patient outcomes and ensuring high-quality care.

Diagnostic Testing and Interpretation

- **Description**: The process of conducting and interpreting diagnostic tests to assess patient conditions.
- **Priority Facts**: Includes understanding the purpose, procedure, and implications of various diagnostic tests.
- **NCLEX Pearls**: Know common laboratory and imaging tests, normal values, and implications of abnormal results.
- **Top Safety Tips**: Ensure correct patient identification, proper test preparation, and timely communication of results.

- **Sample Question**: What is essential for the nurse when preparing a patient for a diagnostic test?
- A. Providing detailed explanations of all possible outcomes.
- B. Ensuring informed consent has been obtained, if necessary.
- C. Administering sedatives routinely before all tests.
- D. Discouraging questions from the patient to avoid anxiety.
- **Correct Answer**: B. Ensuring informed consent has been obtained, if necessary.
- **Rationale**: Informed consent is crucial for any procedure that poses a risk, ensuring that the patient understands the nature and purpose of the test.

4

Pharmacology

Pharmacokinetics and Pharmacodynamics

- **Description**: Pharmacokinetics involves how the body processes a drug (absorption, distribution, metabolism, excretion), while pharmacodynamics deals with how a drug affects the body.
- **Priority Facts**: Understanding these concepts is crucial for safe and effective medication management.
- **NCLEX Pearls**: Be aware of factors like age, liver and kidney function, and drug interactions that can affect pharmacokinetics and pharmacodynamics.
- **Top Safety Tips**: Adjust doses based on patient-specific factors and monitor for therapeutic and adverse effects.
- **Sample Question**: Why is it important to consider a patient's liver function when administering medications?
- A. The liver's role in metabolism can alter the drug's effectiveness and risk of toxicity.
- B. Liver function does not significantly impact drug action or metabolism.
- C. Medications are primarily excreted unchanged in the liver.
- D. All medications are stored in the liver before distribution.
- **Correct Answer**: A. The liver's role in metabolism can alter the drug's

effectiveness and risk of toxicity.
- **Rationale**: The liver metabolizes many drugs; impaired liver function can lead to decreased drug metabolism and increased risk of drug toxicity.

Medication Administration: Routes, Techniques, Safety

- **Description**: The process of administering medications through various routes (oral, intravenous, intramuscular, etc.) and ensuring safety in each method.
- **Priority Facts**: Each route has specific indications, advantages, and techniques.
- **NCLEX Pearls**: Understand the appropriate technique for each route to maximize effectiveness and reduce complications.
- **Top Safety Tips**: Follow the "five rights" of medication administration: right patient, drug, dose, route, and time.
- **Sample Question**: What is a critical safety step before administering oral medication to a patient?
- A. Verifying the patient's preference for liquid or tablet form.
- B. Checking the patient's identification band to ensure correct patient.
- C. Administering the medication without water to ensure absorption.
- D. Giving all the day's medications at once to increase efficiency.
- **Correct Answer**: B. Checking the patient's identification band to ensure correct patient.
- **Rationale**: Verifying the patient's identity is essential to ensure the right patient receives the medication, thereby preventing medication errors.

Drug Classifications and Indications

- **Description**: The categorization of drugs based on their therapeutic use, chemical characteristics, and effects on the body.
- **Priority Facts**: Knowledge of drug classifications helps in understanding the drug's purpose, action, and potential side effects.
- **NCLEX Pearls**: Familiarize yourself with common classes of drugs and

their indications.
- **Top Safety Tips**: Tailor drug therapy based on the specific condition being treated and patient characteristics.
- **Sample Question**: What is the primary indication for administering a beta-blocker?
- A. To increase heart rate in bradycardic patients.
- B. To manage hypertension and prevent angina.
- C. As a first-line treatment for bacterial infections.
- D. To reverse the effects of opioid overdose.
- **Correct Answer**: B. To manage hypertension and prevent angina.
- **Rationale**: Beta-blockers are commonly used to lower blood pressure and reduce the workload on the heart, thus managing hypertension and preventing angina.

Analgesics and Pain Management Medications

- **Description**: Medications used to relieve pain, ranging from mild to severe.
- **Priority Facts**: Includes non-opioid analgesics (like NSAIDs), opioid analgesics, and adjuvant therapies.
- **NCLEX Pearls**: Assess pain levels before and after administration and monitor for side effects.
- **Top Safety Tips**: Be cautious of opioid side effects and the potential for addiction; use non-pharmacological methods when appropriate.
- **Sample Question**: What is important to monitor in a patient receiving opioid analgesics for pain management?
- A. Blood glucose levels.
- B. Respiratory rate and level of consciousness.
- C. Urine output exclusively.
- D. Skin integrity every two weeks.
- **Correct Answer**: B. Respiratory rate and level of consciousness.
- **Rationale**: Opioids can depress the respiratory system; monitoring the respiratory rate and level of consciousness is vital to detect opioid

overdose or severe side effects.

Cardiovascular Medications: Antihypertensives, Diuretics, Anticoagulants

- **Description**: Medications used to manage cardiovascular conditions like hypertension, heart failure, and clotting disorders.
- **Priority Facts**: Antihypertensives manage high blood pressure, diuretics help eliminate excess fluid, and anticoagulants prevent blood clot formation.
- **NCLEX Pearls**: Monitor blood pressure for antihypertensives, electrolyte levels for diuretics, and coagulation parameters for anticoagulants.
- **Top Safety Tips**: Educate about lifestyle changes, adherence to medication regimens, and signs of complications.
- **Sample Question**: What is a key nursing action when administering a loop diuretic?
- A. Encouraging a diet high in potassium.
- B. Restricting fluid intake to enhance diuretic effect.
- C. Monitoring only for increased blood pressure.
- D. Administering the medication before bedtime.
- **Correct Answer**: A. Encouraging a diet high in potassium.
- **Rationale**: Loop diuretics can cause potassium depletion; therefore, monitoring electrolytes and encouraging a potassium-rich diet can help prevent hypokalemia.

Respiratory Medications: Bronchodilators, Corticosteroids

- **Description**: Medications used to treat respiratory conditions like asthma and COPD. Bronchodilators relax muscles in the airways, while corticosteroids reduce inflammation.
- **Priority Facts**: Bronchodilators include beta-agonists and anticholinergics; corticosteroids can be inhaled or systemic.
- **NCLEX Pearls**: Monitor respiratory status before and after administra-

tion, and educate about correct inhaler technique.
- **Top Safety Tips**: Be aware of potential side effects like tachycardia (bronchodilators) and immunosuppression (corticosteroids).
- **Sample Question**: What is critical to teach a patient using inhaled corticosteroids?
- A. Rinse the mouth after each use to prevent oral thrush.
- B. Use the inhaler only during an acute asthma attack.
- C. Discontinue the medication if feeling better.
- D. Combine with a beta-agonist for immediate relief.
- **Correct Answer**: A. Rinse the mouth after each use to prevent oral thrush.
- **Rationale**: Rinsing the mouth after using inhaled corticosteroids helps prevent oral candidiasis (thrush), a common side effect.

Gastrointestinal Medications: Antacids, Laxatives, Antiemetics

- **Description**: Medications that alleviate gastrointestinal symptoms. Antacids neutralize stomach acid, laxatives promote bowel movement, and antiemetics prevent nausea and vomiting.
- **Priority Facts**: Antacids include calcium carbonate and magnesium hydroxide; laxatives can be bulk-forming, stimulant, or osmotic; antiemetics include ondansetron and promethazine.
- **NCLEX Pearls**: Assess for abdominal pain, bowel pattern, and signs of electrolyte imbalance.
- **Top Safety Tips**: Use laxatives cautiously to prevent dependence; monitor for antacid overuse and antiemetic side effects like drowsiness.
- **Sample Question**: What should the nurse monitor for in a patient using osmotic laxatives?
- A. Rapid weight gain.
- B. Signs of dehydration and electrolyte imbalances.
- C. Increased heart rate and blood pressure.
- D. Urinary retention.
- **Correct Answer**: B. Signs of dehydration and electrolyte imbalances.
- **Rationale**: Osmotic laxatives can cause fluid and electrolyte imbalances

due to increased water drawn into the intestines.

Endocrine Medications: Insulins, Oral Hypoglycemics, Thyroid Medications

- **Description**: Medications used to manage endocrine disorders like diabetes and thyroid dysfunction. Insulins and oral hypoglycemics manage blood sugar levels; thyroid medications regulate thyroid function.
- **Priority Facts**: Insulins vary in duration; oral hypoglycemics include sulfonylureas and metformin; thyroid medications include levothyroxine.
- **NCLEX Pearls**: Monitor blood glucose for diabetes medications and thyroid function tests for thyroid medications.
- **Top Safety Tips**: Teach proper insulin injection technique and hypoglycemia recognition; ensure consistent timing of thyroid medication.
- **Sample Question**: What is important when administering levothyroxine?
- A. Administering the medication with meals for better absorption.
- B. Giving the medication at the same time each day, preferably on an empty stomach.
- C. Using alternating sites for injection.
- D. Monitoring for immediate signs of hyperthyroidism post-dose.
- **Correct Answer**: B. Giving the medication at the same time each day, preferably on an empty stomach.
- **Rationale**: Consistent daily dosing of levothyroxine on an empty stomach ensures optimal absorption and effectiveness.

Renal and Urinary Medications: Diuretics, Antispasmodics

- **Description**: Diuretics facilitate the removal of excess fluid from the body; antispasmodics relieve bladder muscle spasms.
- **Priority Facts**: Diuretics include loop, thiazide, and potassium-sparing; antispasmodics include oxybutynin.
- **NCLEX Pearls**: Monitor electrolytes for diuretics, especially potassium levels; watch for urinary retention with antispasmodics.

- **Top Safety Tips**: Educate about signs of electrolyte imbalance and the importance of follow-up labs.
- **Sample Question**: What is a nursing consideration for patients taking loop diuretics?
- A. Encourage a potassium-restricted diet.
- B. Monitor for signs of hypokalemia and dehydration.
- C. Expect increased urinary frequency only during daytime hours.
- D. Administer the medication before bedtime.
- **Correct Answer**: B. Monitor for signs of hypokalemia and dehydration.
- **Rationale**: Loop diuretics can cause potassium loss (hypokalemia) and dehydration due to increased urine production.

Neurological Medications: Anticonvulsants, Antiparkinsonians

- **Description**: Anticonvulsants are used to control seizures; antiparkinsonians manage symptoms of Parkinson's disease.
- **Priority Facts**: Anticonvulsants include drugs like phenytoin and valproic acid; antiparkinsonians include levodopa-carbidopa.
- **NCLEX Pearls**: Monitor for therapeutic levels and side effects; educate about adherence to prevent symptom exacerbation.
- **Top Safety Tips**: Watch for CNS side effects, avoid abrupt withdrawal, and assess for movement disorders.
- **Sample Question**: What is essential when administering anticonvulsants like phenytoin?
- A. Checking the patient's blood pressure post-administration.
- B. Ensuring the drug is administered rapidly IV.
- C. Monitoring plasma drug levels to avoid toxicity.
- D. Administering the drug on an empty stomach for best absorption.
- **Correct Answer**: C. Monitoring plasma drug levels to avoid toxicity.
- **Rationale**: Monitoring plasma levels of phenytoin is essential to ensure therapeutic effectiveness and prevent toxicity, as it has a narrow therapeutic range.

Psychotropic Medications: Antidepressants, Antipsychotics, Anxiolytics

- **Description**: Medications used to treat mental health disorders. Antidepressants manage mood disorders, antipsychotics treat psychotic symptoms, and anxiolytics alleviate anxiety.
- **Priority Facts**: Requires monitoring for effectiveness and side effects like drowsiness, weight gain, or extrapyramidal symptoms.
- **NCLEX Pearls**: Gradual dosage adjustments are often necessary; educate about medication adherence and potential withdrawal symptoms.
- **Top Safety Tips**: Monitor mental status, educate about avoiding alcohol, and assess for suicidal ideation, especially during initial treatment phases.
- **Sample Question**: What is crucial to monitor in a patient newly started on antidepressants?
- A. Immediate improvement in mood.
- B. Signs of increased suicidal thoughts, especially in younger individuals.
- C. Rapid weight loss and decreased appetite.
- D. Development of infectious symptoms like fever or sore throat.
- **Correct Answer**: B. Signs of increased suicidal thoughts, especially in younger individuals.
- **Rationale**: Antidepressants can initially increase suicidal thoughts, particularly in children and young adults; close monitoring during the early stages of treatment is essential.

Anti-Infectives: Antibiotics, Antifungals, Antivirals

- **Description**: Medications used to treat infections. Antibiotics target bacterial infections, antifungals treat fungal infections, and antivirals manage viral infections.
- **Priority Facts**: Requires culture and sensitivity testing for effective treatment; monitor for allergic reactions and medication resistance.
- **NCLEX Pearls**: Ensure correct administration timing and complete the

full course of therapy.
- **Top Safety Tips**: Monitor for side effects like gastrointestinal disturbances and signs of superinfection (e.g., oral thrush).
- **Sample Question**: What is important when administering antibiotics?
- A. Stopping the antibiotic once the patient feels better.
- B. Completing the full course of the prescribed antibiotic.
- C. Using antibiotics as the first line of treatment for viral infections.
- D. Administering probiotics simultaneously to eradicate the infection.
- **Correct Answer**: B. Completing the full course of the prescribed antibiotic.
- **Rationale**: Completing the full course of antibiotics, even if symptoms improve, is crucial to fully eradicate the infection and prevent antibiotic resistance.

Oncology Medications: Chemotherapeutic Agents, Supportive Care Drugs

- **Description**: Medications used in cancer treatment. Chemotherapeutic agents target rapidly dividing cancer cells; supportive care drugs manage side effects and improve quality of life.
- **Priority Facts**: Chemotherapy can cause side effects like nausea, alopecia, and bone marrow suppression.
- **NCLEX Pearls**: Use precautions when handling chemotherapeutic agents and monitor for infusion reactions.
- **Top Safety Tips**: Educate about infection prevention, monitor for neutropenia, and provide supportive care for nausea and vomiting.
- **Sample Question**: What is a key nursing action when administering chemotherapy?
- A. Skipping doses if the patient experiences nausea.
- B. Administering chemotherapy rapidly to reduce exposure time.
- C. Monitoring for signs of an infusion reaction and bone marrow suppression.
- D. Encouraging a high-fiber diet to prevent diarrhea.

- **Correct Answer**: C. Monitoring for signs of an infusion reaction and bone marrow suppression.
- **Rationale**: Due to the toxic nature of chemotherapy, monitoring for infusion reactions and bone marrow suppression is essential to promptly manage adverse effects.

Immunosuppressants and Anti-Inflammatory Agents

- **Description**: Drugs used to suppress the immune system to prevent organ rejection and treat autoimmune conditions; anti-inflammatory agents reduce inflammation and manage pain.
- **Priority Facts**: Immunosuppressants increase the risk of infection; anti-inflammatory agents can cause gastrointestinal upset.
- **NCLEX Pearls**: Monitor for signs of infection and educate about the risks of long-term steroid use.
- **Top Safety Tips**: Advise against live vaccines with immunosuppressants and monitor for adverse effects like cushingoid appearance or osteoporosis.
- **Sample Question**: What is critical for a patient on long-term corticosteroid therapy?
- A. Discontinuing the drug abruptly after long-term use.
- B. Monitoring for signs of infection and bone density changes.
- C. Limiting fluid intake to prevent fluid retention.
- D. Increasing exposure to sunlight for vitamin D synthesis.
- **Correct Answer**: B. Monitoring for signs of infection and bone density changes.
- **Rationale**: Long-term corticosteroid use can suppress the immune response and affect bone density; monitoring for these effects is vital to minimize complications.

Dermatological Medications: Topical Steroids, Antifungals

- **Description**: Medications applied to the skin. Topical steroids reduce inflammation and treat skin conditions; antifungals are used for fungal skin infections.
- **Priority Facts**: Topical steroids vary in potency; overuse can cause skin thinning. Antifungals must be used for the full prescribed duration.
- **NCLEX Pearls**: Apply thin layers of topical steroids; use antifungals as directed.
- **Top Safety Tips**: Monitor for skin changes with prolonged steroid use and ensure complete course of treatment with antifungals.
- **Sample Question**: What is an important consideration when applying topical steroids?
- A. Applying a thick layer for better efficacy.
- B. Using occlusive dressings with every application.
- C. Applying a thin layer to the affected area as prescribed.
- D. Mixing with other creams for enhanced effect.
- **Correct Answer**: C. Applying a thin layer to the affected area as prescribed.
- **Rationale**: A thin layer of topical steroid is sufficient to provide therapeutic effect while minimizing the risk of side effects like skin atrophy.

Ophthalmic and Otic Medications

- **Description**: Medications used for eye and ear conditions. Ophthalmic medications include eye drops and ointments; otic medications include ear drops.
- **Priority Facts**: Used for infections, allergies, glaucoma, and ear infections.
- **NCLEX Pearls**: Proper administration technique is crucial to ensure medication effectiveness.
- **Top Safety Tips**: Avoid touching the tip of the applicator to the eye or

ear; instruct patients on correct self-administration.
- **Sample Question**: What is essential when administering ophthalmic drops?
- A. Placing the drop directly on the cornea.
- B. Instructing the patient to keep their eye closed for 10 minutes post-administration.
- C. Pulling down the lower eyelid and placing the drop in the conjunctival sac.
- D. Shaking the bottle vigorously before administration.
- **Correct Answer**: C. Pulling down the lower eyelid and placing the drop in the conjunctival sac.
- **Rationale**: This technique prevents contamination and ensures the medication is delivered to the correct area without causing discomfort.

Women's Health Medications: Hormonal Therapies, Contraceptives

- **Description**: Medications used in various aspects of women's health, including hormonal replacement therapy and contraceptives.
- **Priority Facts**: Hormonal therapies are used for menopause symptoms, contraception, menstrual issues, and fertility treatment.
- **NCLEX Pearls**: Be aware of contraindications like a history of thromboembolic disorders.
- **Top Safety Tips**: Educate about adherence, potential side effects, and regular follow-ups.
- **Sample Question**: What is an important consideration when prescribing oral contraceptives?
- A. They are suitable for all women regardless of age and medical history.
- B. Monitoring for signs of venous thromboembolism in at-risk patients.
- C. Advising their use only for pregnancy prevention, not for menstrual regulation.
- D. Ensuring immediate discontinuation at the onset of menopause.
- **Correct Answer**: B. Monitoring for signs of venous thromboembolism in at-risk patients.

- **Rationale**: Oral contraceptives can increase the risk of thromboembolic events, particularly in women with certain risk factors. Monitoring for signs is critical for safety.

Pediatric Medications: Dosing and Administration Considerations

- **Description**: The administration of medications in children, requiring specific considerations for dosing and administration.
- **Priority Facts**: Pediatric dosing is often based on weight and age. Liquid formulations are commonly used.
- **NCLEX Pearls**: Double-check dosages with a pediatric dosage calculator and confirm with another healthcare professional if necessary.
- **Top Safety Tips**: Use an oral syringe for liquid medications for accurate dosing; educate caregivers about proper administration and storage.
- **Sample Question**: What is critical when administering medications to a pediatric patient?
- A. Using a kitchen spoon for liquid medications to ensure comfort.
- B. Calculating dose based on the child's weight and confirming with a pharmacist.
- C. Administering adult formulations in smaller volumes.
- D. Relying solely on the child's age to determine the dose.
- **Correct Answer**: B. Calculating dose based on the child's weight and confirming with a pharmacist.
- **Rationale**: Pediatric medication dosages are typically weight-based to ensure safety and efficacy; therefore, accurate calculation and verification are essential.

Geriatric Medications: Polypharmacy and Drug Interactions

- **Description**: Medication management in older adults, often complicated by polypharmacy and increased susceptibility to drug interactions and side effects.
- **Priority Facts**: Geriatric patients may have altered pharmacokinetics due

to age-related changes in metabolism and excretion.
- **NCLEX Pearls**: Regularly review all medications for necessity, appropriate dosing, and potential interactions.
- **Top Safety Tips**: Monitor for adverse drug reactions and educate about medication adherence and potential interactions.
- **Sample Question**: What is a key consideration when managing medications in a geriatric patient?
- A. Prescribing the highest effective dose for quicker results.
- B. Using the same medication regimens as for younger adults.
- C. Regular medication review to minimize polypharmacy risks.
- D. Assuming non-adherence if the medication is not effective.
- **Correct Answer**: C. Regular medication review to minimize polypharmacy risks.
- **Rationale**: Regular reviews help to identify unnecessary medications, adjust dosages, and reduce the risk of adverse drug interactions in older adults.

Emergency Medications: ACLS Drugs, Antidotes

- **Description**: Medications used in emergency settings, including Advanced Cardiac Life Support (ACLS) protocols and antidotes for poisonings.
- **Priority Facts**: Includes drugs like epinephrine, atropine, amiodarone, and various antidotes for specific toxins.
- **NCLEX Pearls**: Familiarity with ACLS protocols and rapid administration of appropriate drugs can be life-saving.
- **Top Safety Tips**: Ensure quick access to emergency drugs, double-check dosages, and monitor patient responses closely.
- **Sample Question**: What is the first-line medication for a patient experiencing cardiac arrest with ventricular fibrillation?
- A. Oral aspirin.
- B. Intravenous amiodarone.
- C. Intramuscular morphine.

- D. Intravenous epinephrine.
- **Correct Answer**: D. Intravenous epinephrine.
- **Rationale**: IV epinephrine is recommended in the management of cardiac arrest due to its vasoconstrictive and cardiac stimulant effects.

Herbal Supplements and Alternative Therapies

- **Description**: Use of plant-derived products and non-mainstream practices for health benefits.
- **Priority Facts**: Includes supplements like St. John's Wort, Echinacea, and ginseng. Efficacy and safety are not always scientifically proven.
- **NCLEX Pearls**: Be aware of potential interactions between herbal supplements and conventional medications.
- **Top Safety Tips**: Obtain a complete health history including all supplements; educate about risks and benefits.
- **Sample Question**: What is important when a patient reports using herbal supplements?
- A. Automatically advising them to stop all supplements.
- B. Assessing for potential interactions with prescribed medications.
- C. Guaranteeing the safety of all natural products.
- D. Ignoring the use of supplements in care planning.
- **Correct Answer**: B. Assessing for potential interactions with prescribed medications.
- **Rationale**: Some herbal supplements can interact with prescription drugs, affecting their efficacy or increasing the risk of adverse effects.

Medication Calculations and Dosage Determinations

- **Description**: The process of calculating correct medication dosages, considering factors like patient weight, age, and drug concentration.
- **Priority Facts**: Accurate calculations are essential for patient safety, especially in vulnerable populations like pediatrics and geriatrics.
- **NCLEX Pearls**: Double-check calculations and confirm with another

healthcare professional if uncertain.
- **Top Safety Tips**: Use appropriate formulas and conversion units; utilize medication calculators as needed.
- **Sample Question**: What is essential when calculating medication dosages for children?
- A. Using adult dosages as a reference point.
- B. Basing dosages on the child's weight and the drug's recommended dose per kilogram.
- C. Administering a standard pediatric dose for all children.
- D. Estimating doses based on the child's age.
- **Correct Answer**: B. Basing dosages on the child's weight and the drug's recommended dose per kilogram.
- **Rationale**: Pediatric dosages are often calculated based on weight to ensure accuracy and safety.

Adverse Drug Reactions and Side Effects

- **Description**: Unintended and sometimes harmful reactions to medications.
- **Priority Facts**: Can range from mild side effects to severe allergic reactions or organ toxicity.
- **NCLEX Pearls**: Monitor patients closely, especially when starting new medications or changing dosages.
- **Top Safety Tips**: Educate patients about potential side effects and when to seek medical attention.
- **Sample Question**: What is a nurse's priority action if a patient experiences an adverse drug reaction?
- A. Continuing the medication to see if the reaction resolves on its own.
- B. Documenting the reaction and notifying the healthcare provider immediately.
- C. Advising the patient to take over-the-counter antihistamines to manage reactions.
- D. Increasing the dosage to overcome the adverse reaction.

- **Correct Answer**: B. Documenting the reaction and notifying the healthcare provider immediately.
- **Rationale**: Prompt documentation and reporting of adverse drug reactions are crucial for patient safety and appropriate management.

Medication Teaching and Compliance

- **Description**: Educating patients about their medications and encouraging adherence to prescribed regimens.
- **Priority Facts**: Includes understanding the purpose, dosage, schedule, side effects, and interactions of medications.
- **NCLEX Pearls**: Use teach-back method to confirm patient understanding; provide written instructions when possible.
- **Top Safety Tips**: Tailor education to patient literacy levels and cultural backgrounds; assess barriers to compliance.
- **Sample Question**: What strategy enhances medication compliance in patients?
- A. Using medical jargon to explain medication benefits and side effects.
- B. Providing detailed, patient-specific education and written instructions.
- C. Advising patients to change their medication regimen if side effects occur.
- D. Recommending online resources for patients to self-educate on medications.
- **Correct Answer**: B. Providing detailed, patient-specific education and written instructions.
- **Rationale**: Personalized education, along with written instructions, helps patients better understand and adhere to their medication regimen, improving outcomes.

5

Pediatric Nursing

Growth and Developmental Stages

- **Description**: A framework for understanding physical, cognitive, and emotional changes that occur from infancy through adolescence.
- **Priority Facts**: Includes milestones for each stage, such as motor skills, language development, and social interactions.
- **NCLEX Pearls**: Use developmental stages to guide assessments, interventions, and anticipatory guidance.
- **Top Safety Tips**: Tailor care to the child's developmental level; use age-appropriate communication and education.
- **Sample Question**: When providing education to a toddler's parents, what developmental characteristic should be considered?
- A. The ability to understand complex reasoning.
- B. Use of abstract concepts to explain health.
- C. Engaging in lengthy discussions about health.
- D. Using simple language and play-based learning.
- **Correct Answer**: D. Using simple language and play-based learning.
- **Rationale**: Toddlers learn best through play and simple, concrete language. This approach is effective for engaging them and ensuring comprehension.

Pediatric Assessment Techniques

- **Description**: Specific methods and approaches used when assessing children, taking into account their developmental stage and communication abilities.
- **Priority Facts**: Techniques vary based on the child's age and developmental level.
- **NCLEX Pearls**: Begin with non-threatening methods; use play and distraction techniques.
- **Top Safety Tips**: Observe for non-verbal cues of distress or pain; involve caregivers in the assessment.
- **Sample Question**: What is a key consideration when performing a physical assessment on a school-age child?
- A. Conducting the assessment in the absence of the parent for accurate responses.
- B. Using medical equipment only after explaining its purpose.
- C. Starting with invasive procedures to quickly gather necessary information.
- D. Relying solely on the child's verbal report for pain assessment.
- **Correct Answer**: B. Using medical equipment only after explaining its purpose.
- **Rationale**: School-age children benefit from understanding the purpose of medical equipment, which reduces anxiety and promotes cooperation.

Common Pediatric Medical Conditions

- **Description**: Typical illnesses and conditions affecting children, such as asthma, otitis media, and common infectious diseases.
- **Priority Facts**: Recognition of common symptoms and appropriate interventions are crucial.
- **NCLEX Pearls**: Familiarize with typical presentation and management of common pediatric conditions.
- **Top Safety Tips**: Educate parents about signs and symptoms that require

medical attention and prevention strategies.
- **Sample Question**: What is a primary nursing action when caring for a child with asthma?
- A. Encouraging vigorous exercise to strengthen lung capacity.
- B. Monitoring respiratory status and administering bronchodilators as prescribed.
- C. Limiting fluid intake to reduce mucus production.
- D. Prescribing antibiotics as a preventive measure.
- **Correct Answer**: B. Monitoring respiratory status and administering bronchodilators as prescribed.
- **Rationale**: Monitoring respiratory status and providing prescribed asthma medications, including bronchodilators, are key to managing asthma in children.

Pediatric Surgical Care

- **Description**: Perioperative nursing care tailored to the specific needs of pediatric patients undergoing surgery.
- **Priority Facts**: Includes preoperative preparation, intraoperative considerations, and postoperative care specific to children.
- **NCLEX Pearls**: Provide age-appropriate education, manage pain effectively, and involve caregivers in the care process.
- **Top Safety Tips**: Monitor for postoperative complications; ensure safety in the recovery room, especially airway management.
- **Sample Question**: What is important when providing postoperative care to a pediatric patient?
- A. Administering pain medication only when the child is crying.
- B. Regular monitoring of vital signs and pain assessment.
- C. Restraining the child to prevent removal of IV lines.
- D. Limiting parental presence to reduce anxiety.
- **Correct Answer**: B. Regular monitoring of vital signs and pain assessment.
- **Rationale**: Regular monitoring of vital signs and pain is essential in

pediatric postoperative care to identify complications early and manage pain effectively.

Pediatric Medication Administration

- **Description**: The process and considerations involved in administering medications to children.
- **Priority Facts**: Pediatric dosages often based on weight; formulations may include liquids, chewables, or dissolvables.
- **NCLEX Pearls**: Verify the correct dose, use an oral syringe for accuracy, and mix liquid medications with a small amount of a favored liquid, if necessary.
- **Top Safety Tips**: Educate caregivers on dosing, storage, and administration techniques.
- **Sample Question**: What is critical to ensure safe medication administration in pediatrics?
- A. Always mixing medications with a large volume of juice or milk.
- B. Using a standardized measuring device, like an oral syringe, for liquid medications.
- C. Adjusting adult doses based on the child's age.
- D. Relying on the child's preference for the medication's flavor.
- **Correct Answer**: B. Using a standardized measuring device, like an oral syringe, for liquid medications.
- **Rationale**: Using an oral syringe ensures accurate dosing of liquid medications, which is vital for safety and effectiveness in pediatric patients.

Pediatric Pain Assessment and Management

- **Description**: Evaluating and treating pain in children, which requires specific approaches due to developmental differences.
- **Priority Facts**: Pain assessment in children often uses scales like the FLACC scale or Wong-Baker FACES scale.
- **NCLEX Pearls**: Recognize that children may express pain differently than adults; non-verbal cues are important.
- **Top Safety Tips**: Use age-appropriate pain management strategies and monitor closely for side effects of pain medications.
- **Sample Question**: What is a key aspect of pediatric pain management?
- A. Administering pain medication only when the child is crying.
- B. Relying solely on the child's verbal report of pain.
- C. Using both pharmacologic and non-pharmacologic pain management techniques.
- D. Avoiding opioids in all pediatric cases due to risk of addiction.
- **Correct Answer**: C. Using both pharmacologic and non-pharmacologic pain management techniques.
- **Rationale**: Combining pharmacologic methods (like medication) with non-pharmacologic (such as distraction, relaxation) provides effective pain management in pediatric patients.

Immunizations and Preventive Care

- **Description**: The administration of vaccines and implementation of preventive measures in pediatric care.
- **Priority Facts**: Follows a schedule recommended by health authorities like the CDC; includes vaccines for diseases like measles, mumps, and pertussis.
- **NCLEX Pearls**: Educate caregivers about vaccine schedules, side effects, and the importance of immunizations.
- **Top Safety Tips**: Screen for contraindications, monitor for reactions post-vaccination, and maintain accurate immunization records.

- **Sample Question**: What is important to verify before administering a vaccine to a pediatric patient?
- A. The child's academic performance.
- B. The child's immunization history and current health status.
- C. Parental employment status.
- D. The child's preference for injection site.
- **Correct Answer**: B. The child's immunization history and current health status.
- **Rationale**: It's crucial to check the child's immunization history and current health to ensure the correct vaccine is administered and to identify any contraindications.

Pediatric Nutrition and Feeding Issues

- **Description**: Addressing the nutritional needs and feeding challenges in infants, children, and adolescents.
- **Priority Facts**: Nutritional needs vary significantly with age and developmental stage; common issues include picky eating, food allergies, and lactose intolerance.
- **NCLEX Pearls**: Assess growth and development regularly, and provide age-appropriate nutritional guidance.
- **Top Safety Tips**: Educate caregivers about healthy eating habits and address feeding issues promptly.
- **Sample Question**: What is a priority when addressing nutritional concerns in a toddler?
- A. Implementing a strict low-fat, low-calorie diet.
- B. Offering a variety of foods and respecting the child's appetite.
- C. Supplementing all meals with high-calorie formulas.
- D. Limiting fluid intake to increase hunger.
- **Correct Answer**: B. Offering a variety of foods and respecting the child's appetite.
- **Rationale**: It's important to offer a variety of foods to toddlers and respect their appetite cues to encourage healthy eating habits and ensure

adequate nutrition.

Genetic and Congenital Disorders

- **Description**: A range of conditions present from birth, either inherited or caused by environmental factors.
- **Priority Facts**: Includes disorders like Down syndrome, cystic fibrosis, and congenital heart defects.
- **NCLEX Pearls**: Understand the specific care requirements and potential complications of common genetic and congenital disorders.
- **Top Safety Tips**: Provide family-centered care, involve multidisciplinary teams, and educate caregivers about long-term management.
- **Sample Question**: What is essential in caring for a child with a congenital heart defect?
- A. Limiting all physical activities to prevent stress on the heart.
- B. Monitoring for signs of heart failure and infection.
- C. Administering prophylactic antibiotics before all medical appointments.
- D. Encouraging a high-sodium diet to increase blood volume.
- **Correct Answer**: B. Monitoring for signs of heart failure and infection.
- **Rationale**: Children with congenital heart defects are at increased risk for heart failure and infection, making close monitoring for these complications essential.

Pediatric Oncology Nursing

- **Description**: Specialized nursing care for children with cancer, including management of chemotherapy and its side effects.
- **Priority Facts**: Pediatric cancers often require aggressive treatment; common types include leukemia, brain tumors, and lymphoma.
- **NCLEX Pearls**: Provide supportive care for side effects of treatment, such as nausea, immunosuppression, and hair loss.
- **Top Safety Tips**: Monitor for infection, manage pain effectively, and

provide emotional support to the child and family.
- **Sample Question**: What is a priority in providing care to a pediatric oncology patient?
- A. Restricting all visitors to minimize infection risk.
- B. Ensuring strict bed rest during treatment periods.
- C. Administering chemotherapy as per protocol and managing side effects.
- D. Focusing solely on physical symptoms and disregarding emotional needs.
- **Correct Answer**: C. Administering chemotherapy as per protocol and managing side effects.
- **Rationale**: Effective administration of chemotherapy and management of its side effects are crucial in pediatric oncology nursing to ensure the child's comfort and treatment efficacy.

Pediatric Neurological Disorders

- **Description**: Conditions affecting the nervous system in children, such as epilepsy, cerebral palsy, and developmental disorders.
- **Priority Facts**: Early detection and intervention are key for optimal outcomes.
- **NCLEX Pearls**: Monitor developmental milestones, assess for neurological deficits, and manage medications for conditions like epilepsy.
- **Top Safety Tips**: Educate caregivers about seizure safety, provide support for developmental needs, and monitor for medication side effects.
- **Sample Question**: What is a priority for a child with epilepsy?
- A. Restricting all physical activities to prevent injury.
- B. Monitoring and managing seizures with appropriate medication.
- C. Keeping the child isolated to reduce stress and seizure triggers.
- D. Administering antiepileptic drugs only after a seizure occurs.
- **Correct Answer**: B. Monitoring and managing seizures with appropriate medication.
- **Rationale**: Effective seizure management with antiepileptic drugs is

crucial in pediatric epilepsy to control seizures and minimize the impact on the child's life.

Pediatric Respiratory Disorders

- **Description**: Respiratory conditions in children, including asthma, cystic fibrosis, and bronchiolitis.
- **Priority Facts**: Symptoms can include coughing, wheezing, and difficulty breathing.
- **NCLEX Pearls**: Understand the signs of respiratory distress and the importance of timely intervention.
- **Top Safety Tips**: Educate about trigger avoidance in asthma, provide chest physiotherapy for cystic fibrosis, and monitor oxygen saturation levels.
- **Sample Question**: What is essential in the management of a child with asthma?
- A. Using bronchodilators only in emergency situations.
- B. Regular use of peak flow meter to monitor asthma control.
- C. Avoiding physical activity to prevent exacerbations.
- D. Administering antibiotics routinely as a preventive measure.
- **Correct Answer**: B. Regular use of peak flow meter to monitor asthma control.
- **Rationale**: Regular monitoring with a peak flow meter helps in managing asthma effectively by detecting changes in airway function.

Pediatric Cardiovascular Disorders

- **Description**: Heart conditions affecting children, such as congenital heart defects, rheumatic heart disease, and Kawasaki disease.
- **Priority Facts**: Early diagnosis and management are vital to prevent long-term complications.
- **NCLEX Pearls**: Monitor heart rate and rhythm, observe for signs of heart failure, and administer cardiac medications as prescribed.

- **Top Safety Tips**: Educate families about signs of cardiac distress and the importance of regular follow-up.
- **Sample Question**: What is important when caring for a child with a congenital heart defect?
- A. Limiting fluid intake drastically to reduce cardiac workload.
- B. Monitoring for signs of heart failure and cyanosis.
- C. Encouraging high-intensity sports for cardiac strengthening.
- D. Administering adult doses of cardiac medications for effectiveness.
- **Correct Answer**: B. Monitoring for signs of heart failure and cyanosis.
- **Rationale**: Children with congenital heart defects are at risk for heart failure and cyanosis; close monitoring for these symptoms is essential for timely intervention.

Pediatric Gastrointestinal Disorders

- **Description**: Disorders of the digestive system in children, such as gastroesophageal reflux disease (GERD), celiac disease, and Hirschsprung's disease.
- **Priority Facts**: Symptoms may include vomiting, diarrhea, constipation, and abdominal pain.
- **NCLEX Pearls**: Assess nutritional status, monitor growth and development, and manage dietary needs specific to the disorder.
- **Top Safety Tips**: Educate caregivers about dietary modifications and signs of complications like dehydration.
- **Sample Question**: What is a key aspect of care for a child with celiac disease?
- A. Implementing a gluten-free diet.
- B. Encouraging a high-fiber diet to manage symptoms.
- C. Administering laxatives regularly for bowel management.
- D. Using corticosteroids as the first-line treatment.
- **Correct Answer**: A. Implementing a gluten-free diet.
- **Rationale**: A gluten-free diet is essential in managing celiac disease, as gluten triggers the immune response that damages the intestines.

Pediatric Renal and Urinary Disorders

- **Description**: Conditions affecting the kidneys and urinary tract in children, like urinary tract infections, nephrotic syndrome, and congenital anomalies.
- **Priority Facts**: Early detection and management can prevent long-term renal damage.
- **NCLEX Pearls**: Monitor urinary output, assess for fluid retention, and manage blood pressure.
- **Top Safety Tips**: Educate about signs of urinary tract infections and the importance of medication adherence in conditions like nephrotic syndrome.
- **Sample Question**: What is crucial in the management of a child with nephrotic syndrome?
- A. Increasing protein intake significantly.
- B. Administering corticosteroids and monitoring for edema.
- C. Limiting fluid intake to minimal amounts.
- D. Using diuretics as the sole treatment modality.
- **Correct Answer**: B. Administering corticosteroids and monitoring for edema.
- **Rationale**: Corticosteroids are commonly used in nephrotic syndrome to reduce inflammation in the kidneys, and monitoring for edema is essential due to fluid retention associated with the condition.

Pediatric Musculoskeletal Disorders

- **Description**: Conditions affecting bones, muscles, and joints in children, such as juvenile arthritis, scoliosis, and fractures.
- **Priority Facts**: Early detection and treatment are crucial to prevent long-term disability.
- **NCLEX Pearls**: Assess for pain, mobility issues, and growth abnormalities.
- **Top Safety Tips**: Educate about safe physical activities, provide pain

management, and monitor for signs of disease progression.
- **Sample Question**: What is essential when caring for a child with juvenile arthritis?
- A. Encouraging complete bed rest during flare-ups.
- B. Administering nonsteroidal anti-inflammatory drugs (NSAIDs) and monitoring joint function.
- C. Avoiding all physical therapy to prevent joint damage.
- D. Focusing solely on dietary changes for treatment.
- **Correct Answer**: B. Administering nonsteroidal anti-inflammatory drugs (NSAIDs) and monitoring joint function.
- **Rationale**: NSAIDs are commonly used to manage pain and inflammation in juvenile arthritis, and monitoring joint function helps assess the disease's progression and treatment effectiveness.

Pediatric Hematologic and Immunologic Disorders

- **Description**: Blood and immune system disorders in children, such as anemia, hemophilia, and immunodeficiency disorders.
- **Priority Facts**: Can affect a child's ability to fight infections and may lead to other health complications.
- **NCLEX Pearls**: Monitor for signs of bleeding, infection, and anemia.
- **Top Safety Tips**: Administer medications like immunoglobulins or clotting factors as prescribed, and educate families on managing risks.
- **Sample Question**: What is a priority nursing intervention for a child with hemophilia?
- A. Encouraging participation in contact sports for social development.
- B. Monitoring for and managing bleeding episodes.
- C. Restricting all physical activity indefinitely.
- D. Administering aspirin for pain relief.
- **Correct Answer**: B. Monitoring for and managing bleeding episodes.
- **Rationale**: Children with hemophilia are at risk for bleeding episodes; monitoring and prompt management of bleeding are critical for their safety.

Pediatric Endocrine Disorders

- **Description**: Endocrine system disorders in children, including diabetes, thyroid disorders, and growth hormone deficiencies.
- **Priority Facts**: Require careful monitoring and management to ensure normal growth and development.
- **NCLEX Pearls**: Administer hormone therapies as prescribed and monitor for effectiveness and side effects.
- **Top Safety Tips**: Educate families on disease management, particularly in lifelong conditions like diabetes.
- **Sample Question**: What is important when managing a child with Type 1 diabetes?
- A. Relying solely on symptoms for blood sugar monitoring.
- B. Regular blood glucose testing and insulin administration.
- C. Limiting carbohydrate intake severely to lower blood sugar.
- D. Using oral hypoglycemics as the primary treatment.
- **Correct Answer**: B. Regular blood glucose testing and insulin administration.
- **Rationale**: Effective management of Type 1 diabetes in children includes regular blood glucose monitoring and administering insulin to manage blood sugar levels.

Child Abuse and Neglect: Identification and Reporting

- **Description**: Recognizing and responding to signs of physical, emotional, sexual abuse, and neglect in children.
- **Priority Facts**: Healthcare providers are legally required to report suspected abuse or neglect.
- **NCLEX Pearls**: Be aware of physical and behavioral indicators of abuse and neglect.
- **Top Safety Tips**: Document findings objectively, report suspicions to the appropriate authorities, and provide supportive care.
- **Sample Question**: What is a nurse's responsibility if child abuse is

suspected?
- A. Confronting the caregiver suspected of abuse.
- B. Reporting the suspicion to child protective services or appropriate authorities.
- C. Waiting for definitive proof before making a report.
- D. Discussing suspicions with the child to confirm the abuse.
- **Correct Answer**: B. Reporting the suspicion to child protective services or appropriate authorities.
- **Rationale**: Nurses are mandated reporters and must report any suspicions of child abuse or neglect to the appropriate authorities, even without definitive proof.

Pediatric Mental Health Disorders

- **Description**: Mental health conditions affecting children, such as attention-deficit/hyperactivity disorder (ADHD), autism spectrum disorders, and anxiety disorders.
- **Priority Facts**: Early intervention can improve outcomes.
- **NCLEX Pearls**: Monitor for behavioral changes, adherence to treatment, and effectiveness of therapy.
- **Top Safety Tips**: Provide a supportive environment, work closely with families and mental health professionals, and educate about medications and therapy.
- **Sample Question**: What is key in the care of a child with ADHD?
- A. Prescribing high doses of stimulant medications immediately.
- B. Providing structured routines and monitoring medication effectiveness.
- C. Restricting all sugar intake to control hyperactivity.
- D. Limiting physical activities to avoid overstimulation.
- **Correct Answer**: B. Providing structured routines and monitoring medication effectiveness.
- **Rationale**: Children with ADHD benefit from structured routines and consistent schedules. Monitoring the effectiveness and side effects

of medications like stimulants is also important for managing ADHD symptoms.

Pediatric Emergency Care

- **Description**: Immediate and efficient care provided to children in emergency situations, including trauma, acute illnesses, and exacerbations of chronic conditions.
- **Priority Facts**: Rapid assessment using the Pediatric Assessment Triangle (Appearance, Work of Breathing, Circulation to the Skin) is crucial.
- **NCLEX Pearls**: Prioritize airway, breathing, and circulation; be aware of the unique anatomical and physiological differences in pediatric patients.
- **Top Safety Tips**: Always consider child abuse as a differential diagnosis, monitor for signs of distress, and maintain a calm environment.
- **Sample Question**: What is the FIRST step in assessing a pediatric patient in the emergency department?
- A. Obtaining a complete health history.
- B. Assessing the child's airway and breathing.
- C. Administering pain medication.
- D. Performing a full neurological exam.
- **Correct Answer**: B. Assessing the child's airway and breathing.
- **Rationale**: In pediatric emergency care, assessment of the airway and breathing is crucial as children are more prone to respiratory distress and failure.

Care of the Hospitalized Child

- **Description**: Nursing care provided to children during hospitalization, addressing both medical and emotional needs.
- **Priority Facts**: Involves managing the child's illness, pain, fear, and separation from family.
- **NCLEX Pearls**: Use developmentally appropriate communication; involve the child and family in care decisions.

- **Top Safety Tips**: Create a safe environment, prevent falls, and closely monitor changes in the child's condition.
- **Sample Question**: What is important when caring for a hospitalized toddler?
- A. Limiting parental presence to encourage independence.
- B. Providing consistent routines and comfort items.
- C. Encouraging the child to make all care decisions.
- D. Restricting play to avoid overexertion.
- **Correct Answer**: B. Providing consistent routines and comfort items.
- **Rationale**: Maintaining consistent routines and having comfort items help to reduce anxiety and provide a sense of security for hospitalized toddlers.

Family Dynamics and Support in Pediatric Nursing

- **Description**: Understanding and supporting the family unit in the context of pediatric nursing.
- **Priority Facts**: Family dynamics greatly influence a child's health and reaction to illness.
- **NCLEX Pearls**: Engage families in care, respect cultural differences, and provide family-centered care.
- **Top Safety Tips**: Communicate openly with family members, provide resources and support, and recognize the impact of a child's illness on the family.
- **Sample Question**: How can nurses effectively support families in pediatric settings?
- A. By making all decisions to alleviate stress on the family.
- B. Encouraging families to stay away to reduce infection risks.
- C. Involving family members in the care and decision-making process.
- D. Providing information only about immediate care and not future planning.
- **Correct Answer**: C. Involving family members in the care and decision-making process.

- **Rationale**: Involving the family in care and decisions respects their role, provides comfort to the child, and ensures a holistic approach to care.

Pediatric Palliative and End-of-Life Care

- **Description**: Specialized care focusing on relieving suffering and improving quality of life for children with life-limiting conditions.
- **Priority Facts**: Involves managing pain and symptoms, and providing emotional support to the child and family.
- **NCLEX Pearls**: Communicate sensitively and honestly; respect the family's wishes and cultural practices.
- **Top Safety Tips**: Focus on comfort care, provide emotional and spiritual support, and coordinate with a multidisciplinary team.
- **Sample Question**: What is a key aspect of providing palliative care to a child?
- A. Focusing only on physical symptoms and ignoring emotional needs.
- B. Providing honest information tailored to the child's developmental level.
- C. Encouraging aggressive treatments regardless of the child's quality of life.
- D. Limiting family involvement to professional healthcare decisions.
- **Correct Answer**: B. Providing honest information tailored to the child's developmental level.
- **Rationale**: Honest, age-appropriate communication is essential in pediatric palliative care to help the child understand their condition and feel supported.

6

Maternity and Women's Health Nursing

Prenatal Care and Assessments

- **Description**: Care provided to expectant mothers throughout pregnancy to ensure the health of both mother and fetus.
- **Priority Facts**: Includes regular monitoring of fetal development, maternal health checks, and screening tests.
- **NCLEX Pearls**: Understand the significance of each prenatal visit, monitor for gestational diabetes and preeclampsia.
- **Top Safety Tips**: Educate about healthy lifestyle choices, recognize signs of potential complications, and ensure timely follow-up.
- **Sample Question**: What is a key component of prenatal care?
- A. Limiting all physical activity throughout pregnancy.
- B. Conducting regular assessments of fetal development and maternal well-being.
- C. Administering over-the-counter medications for any discomfort.
- D. Performing ultrasound at every prenatal visit.
- **Correct Answer**: B. Conducting regular assessments of fetal development and maternal well-being.
- **Rationale**: Regular assessments are vital in prenatal care for monitoring the progress of pregnancy and identifying any potential health concerns.

Labor and Delivery Processes

- **Description**: The process of childbirth, including the stages of labor and delivery methods.
- **Priority Facts**: Labor is divided into three stages: dilation, expulsion, and placental delivery.
- **NCLEX Pearls**: Monitor maternal and fetal well-being, manage pain, and prepare for potential interventions.
- **Top Safety Tips**: Recognize signs of labor progression and complications, such as fetal distress or prolonged labor.
- **Sample Question**: What is crucial when managing a woman in active labor?
- A. Encouraging the mother to hold her breath during contractions.
- B. Monitoring fetal heart rate and maternal vital signs regularly.
- C. Delaying pain relief measures until the final stage of labor.
- D. Insisting on a specific birthing position regardless of comfort.
- **Correct Answer**: B. Monitoring fetal heart rate and maternal vital signs regularly.
- **Rationale**: Regular monitoring of fetal heart rate and maternal vitals is essential to assess the well-being of both mother and baby during labor.

Postpartum Nursing Care

- **Description**: Care provided to the mother following childbirth to ensure recovery and promote family bonding.
- **Priority Facts**: Focuses on physical recovery, emotional support, breastfeeding assistance, and newborn care education.
- **NCLEX Pearls**: Monitor for postpartum complications like hemorrhage, infection, and depression.
- **Top Safety Tips**: Assess for uterine atony, provide pain management, and support breastfeeding.
- **Sample Question**: What is a priority in postpartum nursing care?
- A. Restricting fluid intake to prevent edema.

- B. Monitoring for signs of postpartum hemorrhage and infection.
- C. Encouraging immediate return to pre-pregnancy activities.
- D. Limiting infant-mother interaction to promote rest.
- **Correct Answer**: B. Monitoring for signs of postpartum hemorrhage and infection.
- **Rationale**: Vigilant monitoring for postpartum hemorrhage and infection is crucial for early detection and management, ensuring the safety and well-being of the mother.

Neonatal Nursing Care

- **Description**: Specialized care provided to newborns in the first few weeks of life.
- **Priority Facts**: Includes assessment of vital signs, feeding support, jaundice monitoring, and parent education.
- **NCLEX Pearls**: Understand normal newborn physiology and the signs of common neonatal complications.
- **Top Safety Tips**: Maintain thermoregulation, monitor for feeding difficulties, and educate parents on newborn care.
- **Sample Question**: What is an important aspect of neonatal nursing care?
- A. Keeping the newborn in a separate nursery at all times for rest.
- B. Ensuring proper thermoregulation and monitoring for jaundice.
- C. Feeding the newborn only when it cries to establish a routine.
- D. Avoiding all parental contact to reduce infection risk.
- **Correct Answer**: B. Ensuring proper thermoregulation and monitoring for jaundice.
- **Rationale**: Newborns are at risk for hypothermia and jaundice; thus, maintaining proper body temperature and monitoring skin and sclera color are important for neonatal care.

High-Risk Pregnancies and Complications

- **Description**: Management of pregnancies with increased risk for maternal and/or fetal complications.
- **Priority Facts**: Includes conditions like preeclampsia, gestational diabetes, preterm labor, and placenta previa.
- **NCLEX Pearls**: Closely monitor for signs of worsening conditions, manage maternal health, and prepare for potential early delivery.
- **Top Safety Tips**: Provide targeted education about warning signs, ensure adherence to treatment plans, and coordinate care with specialists.
- **Sample Question**: What is essential when caring for a woman with preeclampsia?
- A. Implementing a strict low-sodium diet exclusively.
- B. Monitoring blood pressure and signs of severe headache or visual changes.
- C. Encouraging vigorous exercise to lower blood pressure.
- D. Discontinuing prenatal vitamins to reduce blood pressure.
- **Correct Answer**: B. Monitoring blood pressure and signs of severe headache or visual changes.
- **Rationale**: Preeclampsia can progress rapidly; monitoring blood pressure and symptoms like headache or visual changes is key to managing and detecting severe cases.

Fetal Assessment and Monitoring

- **Description**: Techniques used to evaluate fetal health and development during pregnancy and labor.
- **Priority Facts**: Includes fetal heart rate monitoring, ultrasound, non-stress tests, and biophysical profiles.
- **NCLEX Pearls**: Recognize patterns indicating fetal distress, such as bradycardia or tachycardia.

- **Top Safety Tips**: Interpret fetal monitoring data accurately and respond promptly to signs of distress.
- **Sample Question**: During labor, what indicates a need for immediate nursing intervention in fetal heart rate monitoring?
- A. A baseline rate of 120-160 beats per minute.
- B. Regular accelerations with fetal movement.
- C. Persistent late decelerations.
- D. Brief early decelerations coinciding with contractions.
- **Correct Answer**: C. Persistent late decelerations.
- **Rationale**: Late decelerations may indicate uteroplacental insufficiency, requiring immediate assessment and potential intervention.

Breastfeeding and Newborn Nutrition

- **Description**: Supporting and managing infant feeding, including breastfeeding and formula feeding.
- **Priority Facts**: Breastfeeding provides optimal nutrition and immunity; formula is an alternative when breastfeeding is not possible.
- **NCLEX Pearls**: Assist with latch-on techniques, monitor infant weight gain, and address common breastfeeding challenges.
- **Top Safety Tips**: Educate about feeding cues, proper formula preparation, and storage.
- **Sample Question**: What is a key nursing action to support successful breastfeeding?
- A. Advising mothers to use formula as a supplement routinely.
- B. Encouraging breastfeeding on a strict schedule.
- C. Assisting with proper latch and positioning techniques.
- D. Limiting breastfeeding duration to 10 minutes per breast.
- **Correct Answer**: C. Assisting with proper latch and positioning techniques.
- **Rationale**: Proper latch and positioning are crucial for effective breastfeeding and preventing problems like nipple soreness and inadequate milk transfer.

Common Gynecological Disorders

- **Description**: Disorders affecting the female reproductive system, such as endometriosis, polycystic ovary syndrome (PCOS), and uterine fibroids.
- **Priority Facts**: Symptoms can include pelvic pain, menstrual irregularities, and infertility.
- **NCLEX Pearls**: Assess for symptoms, educate about treatment options, and manage pain.
- **Top Safety Tips**: Provide emotional support, discuss reproductive implications, and monitor for complications.
- **Sample Question**: What is important in the care of a patient with PCOS?
- A. Implementing a carbohydrate-rich diet.
- B. Advising total avoidance of exercise.
- C. Monitoring for metabolic complications and providing lifestyle education.
- D. Guaranteeing pregnancy with fertility treatments.
- **Correct Answer**: C. Monitoring for metabolic complications and providing lifestyle education.
- **Rationale**: PCOS is often associated with metabolic complications like insulin resistance; lifestyle modifications can be key in managing symptoms.

Women's Health: Preventive Care and Screenings

- **Description**: Regular check-ups and screenings to prevent and detect health issues in women, such as cervical and breast cancer.
- **Priority Facts**: Includes Pap smears, mammography, bone density tests, and routine physical exams.
- **NCLEX Pearls**: Educate about the importance and frequency of screenings based on age and risk factors.
- **Top Safety Tips**: Ensure timely follow-up on abnormal results and provide guidance on health maintenance.
- **Sample Question**: What is a primary aspect of preventive care in women's

health?
- A. Performing mammograms annually starting at age 20.
- B. Encouraging self-breast exams as the sole screening for breast cancer.
- C. Scheduling regular health screenings like Pap smears and mammograms.
- D. Limiting physical examinations to postmenopausal women.
- **Correct Answer**: C. Scheduling regular health screenings like Pap smears and mammograms.
- **Rationale**: Regular screenings such as Pap smears and mammograms are essential for early detection of conditions like cervical and breast cancer.

Contraception and Family Planning

- **Description**: Advising on and managing various contraceptive methods to plan and prevent pregnancy.
- **Priority Facts**: Includes birth control pills, intrauterine devices (IUDs), condoms, and sterilization.
- **NCLEX Pearls**: Discuss options considering medical history, lifestyle, and personal preferences.
- **Top Safety Tips**: Educate about proper use, potential side effects, and what to do in case of missed doses.
- **Sample Question**: What is important when discussing contraceptive options with a patient?
- A. Recommending the same method for all women for consistency.
- B. Assessing individual needs, lifestyle, and health status to determine the best fit.
- C. Discouraging discussion about sexual health as it is a sensitive topic.
- D. Focusing solely on permanent methods for long-term planning.
- **Correct Answer**: B. Assessing individual needs, lifestyle, and health status to determine the best fit.
- **Rationale**: Contraceptive needs vary; individualized assessment ensures that the chosen method aligns with the patient's health, lifestyle, and family planning goals.

Menopausal Care and Hormone Replacement Therapy

- **Description**: Management of menopausal symptoms and health considerations, including the use of hormone replacement therapy (HRT).
- **Priority Facts**: Addresses symptoms like hot flashes, night sweats, mood changes, and osteoporosis risk.
- **NCLEX Pearls**: Evaluate the risks and benefits of HRT, considering individual patient factors.
- **Top Safety Tips**: Monitor for side effects of HRT, such as thromboembolic events and breast cancer risk.
- **Sample Question**: What is essential to assess before initiating hormone replacement therapy in a menopausal woman?
- A. The patient's preference for tablet or liquid medication forms.
- B. Personal and family medical history, including risk factors for breast cancer and cardiovascular disease.
- C. The patient's ability to purchase over-the-counter supplements.
- D. The patient's level of physical activity and diet preferences.
- **Correct Answer**: B. Personal and family medical history, including risk factors for breast cancer and cardiovascular disease.
- **Rationale**: Assessing personal and family history is critical to determining the appropriateness of HRT and balancing the benefits against potential risks.

Maternal and Newborn Medications

- **Description**: Medications used during pregnancy, labor, delivery, and for newborn care.
- **Priority Facts**: Includes prenatal vitamins, analgesics during labor, antibiotics for Group B strep, and vaccinations for newborns.
- **NCLEX Pearls**: Be aware of medication effects on the fetus and newborn, and adjust dosages accordingly.
- **Top Safety Tips**: Administer medications considering pregnancy and breastfeeding status; monitor for adverse reactions in both mother and

newborn.
- **Sample Question**: When administering medications to a breastfeeding mother, what is important to consider?
- A. Stopping breastfeeding when any medication is prescribed.
- B. The potential for medication transfer to breast milk and its effects on the infant.
- C. Using adult medications as they are deemed safer than pediatric formulations.
- D. Encouraging formula feeding as a safer alternative to breast milk when medicated.
- **Correct Answer**: B. The potential for medication transfer to breast milk and its effects on the infant.
- **Rationale**: Understanding how medications can affect breast milk and the nursing infant is crucial for safe breastfeeding while medicated.

Perinatal Loss and Grief Support

- **Description**: Providing compassionate care and support to families experiencing perinatal loss, including miscarriage, stillbirth, or neonatal death.
- **Priority Facts**: Involves emotional support, empathy, and understanding of the grieving process.
- **NCLEX Pearls**: Offer sensitive communication, acknowledge the loss, and provide resources for grief counseling.
- **Top Safety Tips**: Create a supportive environment, respect family's wishes for mourning practices, and provide physical care as needed.
- **Sample Question**: What is a nurse's role in supporting parents during perinatal loss?
- A. Encouraging quick emotional recovery to decrease distress.
- B. Providing a quiet space for parents to grieve and offering emotional support.
- C. Avoiding discussion of the loss to reduce trauma.
- D. Immediately focusing on future pregnancy planning.

- **Correct Answer**: B. Providing a quiet space for parents to grieve and offering emotional support.
- **Rationale**: Offering a private space and emotional support respects the parents' need to grieve and process their loss at their own pace.

Women's Health Education and Counseling

- **Description**: Educating women about health issues, preventive care, reproductive health, and lifestyle choices.
- **Priority Facts**: Includes topics like sexual health, cervical and breast cancer screenings, contraception, and healthy lifestyle practices.
- **NCLEX Pearls**: Tailor education to individual needs and cultural backgrounds; use clear, understandable language.
- **Top Safety Tips**: Encourage open communication, respect confidentiality, and provide evidence-based information.
- **Sample Question**: What is key in providing effective women's health education?
- A. Delivering all education in a group setting for efficiency.
- B. Using medical jargon to emphasize the importance of health issues.
- C. Assessing individual health literacy and providing tailored education.
- D. Focusing solely on reproductive health, regardless of age or interest.
- **Correct Answer**: C. Assessing individual health literacy and providing tailored education.
- **Rationale**: Personalizing health education based on the woman's health literacy, needs, and concerns ensures the information is understood and relevant.

7

Mental Health and Psychiatric Nursing

Mental Health Assessment and Diagnosis

- **Description**: Process of evaluating psychological, emotional, and behavioral symptoms to diagnose mental health conditions.
- **Priority Facts**: Involves the use of standardized assessment tools, clinical interviews, and observation.
- **NCLEX Pearls**: Be aware of signs and symptoms of common mental health disorders; understand the importance of a holistic approach.
- **Top Safety Tips**: Maintain a nonjudgmental attitude, ensure patient safety during assessment, and respect confidentiality.
- **Sample Question**: What is a crucial element in conducting a mental health assessment?
- A. Relying solely on family reports for diagnosis.
- B. Using open-ended questions to gather comprehensive information about the patient's symptoms.
- C. Focusing exclusively on physical symptoms presented by the patient.
- D. Diagnosing based on a single symptom without a thorough evaluation.
- **Correct Answer**: B. Using open-ended questions to gather comprehensive information about the patient's symptoms.
- **Rationale**: Open-ended questions allow for a more comprehensive

understanding of the patient's symptoms and experiences, crucial for accurate assessment and diagnosis.

Therapeutic Communication and Relationship Building

- **Description**: Techniques used in mental health nursing to establish rapport and provide support to patients.
- **Priority Facts**: Involves active listening, empathy, and the use of open-ended questions.
- **NCLEX Pearls**: Establish trust, respect boundaries, and avoid judgmental responses.
- **Top Safety Tips**: Be aware of verbal and nonverbal cues, maintain professional boundaries, and ensure a safe environment.
- **Sample Question**: What is key in building a therapeutic relationship with a mental health patient?
- A. Providing advice based on personal experiences.
- B. Establishing trust and understanding through empathetic listening and respect.
- C. Agreeing with all patient statements to avoid confrontation.
- D. Focusing on rapid symptom resolution rather than relationship building.
- **Correct Answer**: B. Establishing trust and understanding through empathetic listening and respect.
- **Rationale**: Trust and understanding, fostered by empathetic listening and respect, are foundational in building effective therapeutic relationships in mental health care.

Anxiety and Mood Disorders

- **Description**: A group of mental health conditions characterized by significant anxiety or mood disturbances, such as depression and bipolar disorder.
- **Priority Facts**: Symptoms can impact daily functioning and quality of

life.
- **NCLEX Pearls**: Recognize symptoms, provide support, and understand medication management.
- **Top Safety Tips**: Monitor for suicidal ideation, particularly in the early stages of treatment, and educate about coping strategies.
- **Sample Question**: What is an essential nursing intervention for a patient with major depressive disorder?
- A. Encouraging the patient to avoid social interactions until symptoms improve.
- B. Monitoring for changes in mood and response to treatment.
- C. Withholding all medications until a positive mood is consistently observed.
- D. Assuring the patient that symptoms will resolve without intervention.
- **Correct Answer**: B. Monitoring for changes in mood and response to treatment.
- **Rationale**: Monitoring mood and treatment response is crucial in managing major depressive disorder, particularly for identifying treatment effectiveness and any emergent suicidal ideation.

Schizophrenia and Other Psychotic Disorders

- **Description**: Mental health conditions characterized by alterations in thinking, perception, and behavior.
- **Priority Facts**: Symptoms include hallucinations, delusions, disorganized thinking, and impaired social functioning.
- **NCLEX Pearls**: Understand the chronic nature of these disorders and the importance of medication adherence.
- **Top Safety Tips**: Monitor for medication side effects, provide reality orientation, and ensure a safe environment.
- **Sample Question**: What is a priority nursing action for a patient experiencing hallucinations?
- A. Immediately confronting and arguing against the hallucinations.
- B. Acknowledging the patient's experience and providing a reality-based

orientation.
- C. Isolating the patient to prevent stress-induced hallucinations.
- D. Encouraging the patient to interpret the meaning of the hallucinations.
- **Correct Answer**: B. Acknowledging the patient's experience and providing a reality-based orientation.
- **Rationale**: Acknowledging the patient's experiences while gently orienting them to reality helps in managing hallucinations without invalidating the patient's experience.

Personality and Impulse Control Disorders

- **Description**: Disorders characterized by enduring patterns of behavior, cognition, and inner experience that deviate from cultural expectations.
- **Priority Facts**: Includes disorders like borderline personality disorder and antisocial personality disorder.
- **NCLEX Pearls**: Be consistent, set clear boundaries, and manage challenging behaviors effectively.
- **Top Safety Tips**: Monitor for self-harm or risky behaviors, provide structured interactions, and maintain clear and consistent limits.
- **Sample Question**: How should a nurse manage care for a patient with borderline personality disorder?
- A. Establishing flexible boundaries to accommodate the patient's mood swings.
- B. Reacting personally to the patient's behaviors and comments.
- C. Maintaining consistent boundaries and a structured environment.
- D. Isolating the patient from others to reduce relational conflicts.
- **Correct Answer**: C. Maintaining consistent boundaries and a structured environment.
- **Rationale**: Consistent boundaries and a structured approach are essential in managing patients with borderline personality disorder, as they help to provide stability and reduce manipulative behaviors.

Substance Use and Addictive Disorders

- **Description**: Disorders characterized by the excessive use of substances like alcohol, opioids, and stimulants, leading to significant impairment or distress.
- **Priority Facts**: Includes physical dependence, withdrawal symptoms, and the impact on daily life.
- **NCLEX Pearls**: Screen for substance use, provide nonjudgmental support, and understand detoxification processes.
- **Top Safety Tips**: Monitor for withdrawal symptoms, provide appropriate referrals, and educate about relapse prevention.
- **Sample Question**: What is a priority nursing action for a patient undergoing opioid withdrawal?
- A. Encouraging the patient to resume substance use at lower doses to prevent withdrawal.
- B. Monitoring vital signs and administering prescribed medication to manage withdrawal symptoms.
- C. Isolating the patient to prevent disturbances to other patients.
- D. Implementing physical restraints to prevent self-harm.
- **Correct Answer**: B. Monitoring vital signs and administering prescribed medication to manage withdrawal symptoms.
- **Rationale**: Close monitoring and medical management of withdrawal symptoms are essential in safely managing opioid withdrawal.

Eating Disorders

- **Description**: Conditions characterized by abnormal or disturbed eating habits, such as anorexia nervosa and bulimia nervosa.
- **Priority Facts**: Can lead to severe physical health problems and are often associated with psychological issues.
- **NCLEX Pearls**: Be aware of the signs of eating disorders and the importance of a multidisciplinary approach to treatment.
- **Top Safety Tips**: Monitor nutritional status, provide emotional support,

and educate about healthy eating behaviors.
- **Sample Question**: What is an important aspect of care for a patient with anorexia nervosa?
- A. Focusing solely on rapid weight gain as a measure of recovery.
- B. Collaborating with dietitians, therapists, and the patient for a holistic treatment approach.
- C. Encouraging the patient to exercise as a method to improve mood.
- D. Implementing strict dietary restrictions to regain control over eating habits.
- **Correct Answer**: B. Collaborating with dietitians, therapists, and the patient for a holistic treatment approach.
- **Rationale**: A holistic approach involving a multidisciplinary team is crucial in treating anorexia nervosa, addressing both the physical and psychological aspects of the disorder.

Child and Adolescent Mental Health Disorders

- **Description**: A range of mental health conditions affecting children and adolescents, including ADHD, autism spectrum disorders, and depression.
- **Priority Facts**: Early intervention can significantly improve outcomes.
- **NCLEX Pearls**: Tailor assessments and interventions to the developmental level; involve family in care.
- **Top Safety Tips**: Monitor for changes in behavior or mood, encourage consistent routines, and provide age-appropriate education.
- **Sample Question**: What is essential when caring for a child with ADHD?
- A. Administering medications only during school hours.
- B. Consistently applying behavioral strategies and monitoring for side effects of medication.
- C. Using punishment to manage inattentive or hyperactive behaviors.
- D. Limiting all screen time to prevent overstimulation.
- **Correct Answer**: B. Consistently applying behavioral strategies and monitoring for side effects of medication.

- **Rationale**: Consistent application of behavioral strategies, along with careful monitoring of medication effects, is key in managing ADHD in children and adolescents.

Elderly Mental Health Issues

- **Description**: Mental health disorders in older adults, including dementia, depression, and anxiety disorders.
- **Priority Facts**: Conditions may be complicated by comorbidities and age-related changes.
- **NCLEX Pearls**: Screen for cognitive impairment, address age-specific concerns, and involve caregivers in care.
- **Top Safety Tips**: Monitor for medication side effects, provide a safe environment, and encourage social engagement.
- **Sample Question**: What is a priority when providing care for an elderly patient with depression?
- A. Assuming depression is a normal part of aging and limiting interventions.
- B. Monitoring for signs of depression worsening and encouraging participation in therapy.
- C. Focusing exclusively on pharmacological treatment without considering psychotherapy.
- D. Discouraging discussions about feelings to prevent exacerbating the depression.
- **Correct Answer**: B. Monitoring for signs of depression worsening and encouraging participation in therapy.
- **Rationale**: Recognizing that depression is not a normal part of aging and actively monitoring and treating it, including encouraging participation in therapy, is essential in elderly care.

Psychiatric Medications and Side Effects

- **Description**: Medications used in the treatment of psychiatric disorders and their potential side effects.
- **Priority Facts**: Includes antidepressants, antipsychotics, mood stabilizers, and anxiolytics.
- **NCLEX Pearls**: Understand the indications for use, potential side effects, and the importance of medication adherence.
- **Top Safety Tips**: Monitor for adverse effects, provide education about medication management, and assess for interactions with other medications.
- **Sample Question**: What is essential to monitor in a patient starting a new antipsychotic medication?
- A. Only focusing on improvement of symptoms and disregarding potential side effects.
- B. Side effects like weight gain, metabolic changes, and extrapyramidal symptoms.
- C. Encouraging cessation of the medication if any side effect occurs.
- D. Limiting fluid intake to prevent side effects like edema.
- **Correct Answer**: B. Side effects like weight gain, metabolic changes, and extrapyramidal symptoms.
- **Rationale**: Monitoring for common side effects of antipsychotic medications, such as weight gain, metabolic syndrome, and extrapyramidal symptoms, is crucial to manage these effects and ensure patient safety.

Suicide Risk Assessment and Prevention

- **Description**: Evaluating the risk factors and warning signs of suicide, and implementing strategies to prevent suicidal behavior.
- **Priority Facts**: Key risk factors include previous suicide attempts, mental health disorders, substance abuse, and significant life changes.
- **NCLEX Pearls**: Take any talk of suicide seriously, conduct thorough risk assessments, and develop safety plans.

- **Top Safety Tips**: Maintain a safe environment, establish strong therapeutic relationships, and ensure constant monitoring if risk is high.
- **Sample Question**: What is the MOST important action when a patient expresses suicidal thoughts?
- A. Assuming the patient is seeking attention and not taking the comments seriously.
- B. Immediately implementing safety precautions and conducting a detailed risk assessment.
- C. Leaving the patient alone to provide space to calm down.
- D. Telling the patient that things will improve without specific interventions.
- **Correct Answer**: B. Immediately implementing safety precautions and conducting a detailed risk assessment.
- **Rationale**: Immediate response to suicidal ideation, including safety measures and a comprehensive risk assessment, is essential to prevent potential suicide attempts and ensure patient safety.

Crisis Intervention and Acute Psychiatric Care

- **Description**: Immediate and short-term care provided in psychiatric emergencies to stabilize individuals.
- **Priority Facts**: Involves managing acute mental health crises like severe anxiety, psychosis, or behavioral disturbances.
- **NCLEX Pearls**: Use de-escalation techniques, assess for immediate risks, and provide supportive care.
- **Top Safety Tips**: Prioritize patient safety, avoid escalating situations, and coordinate with multidisciplinary teams for comprehensive care.
- **Sample Question**: What is a key nursing intervention in acute psychiatric crisis management?
- A. Using physical restraints as a first-line intervention.
- B. Immediately administering high-dose psychotropic medications.
- C. Engaging in active listening and employing de-escalation techniques.
- D. Isolating the patient from all stimuli until the crisis resolves.

- **Correct Answer**: C. Engaging in active listening and employing de-escalation techniques.
- **Rationale**: Active listening and de-escalation techniques are critical in managing acute psychiatric crises, helping to calm the patient and assess needs without escalating the situation.

Group and Family Therapy in Mental Health

- **Description**: Therapeutic approaches involving multiple patients or family members to address mental health issues.
- **Priority Facts**: Group therapy fosters shared experiences and support; family therapy addresses dynamics affecting mental health.
- **NCLEX Pearls**: Understand group dynamics, facilitate open communication, and respect confidentiality.
- **Top Safety Tips**: Monitor interactions to ensure a safe and respectful environment and address any counterproductive behaviors.
- **Sample Question**: What is an important role of the nurse in a mental health group therapy session?
- A. Allowing one member to dominate the session to encourage their participation.
- B. Facilitating discussion and ensuring respectful interaction among group members.
- C. Sharing personal experiences to encourage openness in the group.
- D. Focusing solely on the most vocal members and their issues.
- **Correct Answer**: B. Facilitating discussion and ensuring respectful interaction among group members.
- **Rationale**: Facilitating balanced discussion and ensuring respectful interactions are crucial in group therapy to provide a safe and therapeutic environment for all participants.

Legal and Ethical Issues in Psychiatric Nursing

- **Description**: Understanding and adhering to legal and ethical standards in psychiatric nursing practice.
- **Priority Facts**: Includes patient rights, consent for treatment, confidentiality, and mandatory reporting.
- **NCLEX Pearls**: Stay informed about legal and ethical guidelines, including involuntary commitments and patients' rights.
- **Top Safety Tips**: Always prioritize patient safety, obtain informed consent when applicable, and maintain confidentiality.
- **Sample Question**: What is critical to consider regarding legal and ethical issues in psychiatric nursing?
- A. Ignoring patients' rights if they are deemed incompetent.
- B. Sharing patient information with anyone interested in the patient's well-being.
- C. Adhering to principles of confidentiality, informed consent, and patient autonomy.
- D. Making treatment decisions based solely on the nurse's judgment.
- **Correct Answer**: C. Adhering to principles of confidentiality, informed consent, and patient autonomy.
- **Rationale**: Upholding ethical principles like confidentiality, informed consent, and respecting patient autonomy is essential in psychiatric nursing to ensure legal compliance and ethical care delivery.

Community Mental Health Nursing

- **Description**: Nursing practice focused on promoting mental health and providing care in community settings, such as clinics, homes, and schools.
- **Priority Facts**: Involves outreach, early intervention, crisis management, and collaboration with community resources.
- **NCLEX Pearls**: Be aware of cultural and socio-economic factors affecting mental health; provide accessible care tailored to community needs.

- **Top Safety Tips**: Ensure continuity of care, monitor for signs of relapse or crisis, and maintain strong links with local mental health services.
- **Sample Question**: What is essential for a nurse working in community mental health?
- A. Focusing solely on medication management for psychiatric conditions.
- B. Providing holistic care, including assessment of social, economic, and environmental factors.
- C. Limiting care to only severe mental health conditions and referring others to specialized care.
- D. Advising patients to avoid community resources for fear of stigmatization.
- **Correct Answer**: B. Providing holistic care, including assessment of social, economic, and environmental factors.
- **Rationale**: Holistic care in community mental health nursing addresses not just the clinical aspects of mental health but also social, economic, and environmental factors that can impact mental well-being.

Mental Health Promotion and Education

- **Description**: Strategies to enhance mental health awareness and promote psychological well-being in the general population.
- **Priority Facts**: Includes education on stress management, resilience building, and recognition of mental health disorders.
- **NCLEX Pearls**: Use evidence-based information to educate the public; address myths and stigma associated with mental health.
- **Top Safety Tips**: Provide accurate information, encourage healthy lifestyle choices, and promote accessible mental health resources.
- **Sample Question**: What is a key aspect of mental health promotion and education by nurses?
- A. Discouraging discussions about mental health to avoid causing anxiety.
- B. Promoting awareness and understanding of mental health issues and resources.
- C. Focusing only on high-risk groups and ignoring the broader commu-

nity.
- D. Providing education exclusively on medication management for mental health conditions.
- **Correct Answer**: B. Promoting awareness and understanding of mental health issues and resources.
- **Rationale**: Educating the public about mental health, including awareness of conditions and available resources, is crucial in promoting mental well-being and reducing stigma.

8

Gerontological Nursing

Geriatric Assessment and Care Planning

- **Description**: Comprehensive evaluation of physical, psychological, and functional capabilities of older adults to develop a coordinated and integrated plan for treatment and long-term follow-up.
- **Priority Facts**: Includes assessment of mobility, cognition, nutrition, and social support.
- **NCLEX Pearls**: Tailor assessments to the individual's needs, considering age-related changes.
- **Top Safety Tips**: Consider polypharmacy risks, identify fall risks, and ensure clear communication with caregivers.
- **Sample Question**: What is crucial in the geriatric assessment for care planning?
- A. Relying on family members to provide all patient history information.
- B. Conducting a thorough multidimensional assessment to guide care planning.
- C. Focusing solely on physical health issues, ignoring cognitive and emotional aspects.
- D. Using the same assessment approach as for younger adult patients.
- **Correct Answer**: B. Conducting a thorough multidimensional assessment

to guide care planning.
- **Rationale**: A comprehensive multidimensional assessment is key in geriatrics to address the complex needs of older adults, including physical, cognitive, and psychosocial aspects.

Common Health Issues in Older Adults

- **Description**: Age-related health conditions commonly seen in the geriatric population, such as arthritis, cardiovascular diseases, and sensory impairments.
- **Priority Facts**: Management often involves addressing multiple coexisting conditions.
- **NCLEX Pearls**: Be aware of the atypical presentation of diseases in older adults.
- **Top Safety Tips**: Monitor for adverse drug reactions, and provide patient education on disease management.
- **Sample Question**: What is important when managing multiple health issues in older adults?
- A. Prescribing medications without considering potential interactions.
- B. Assessing for interactions and complications of multiple health conditions.
- C. Focusing treatment on the most severe condition only.
- D. Ignoring the patient's preferences in treatment decisions.
- **Correct Answer**: B. Assessing for interactions and complications of multiple health conditions.
- **Rationale**: Considering the interactions and complications of multiple conditions is essential in providing holistic and safe care for older adults with multiple health issues.

Geriatric Syndromes: Falls, Incontinence, Delirium

- **Description**: Common complex conditions in older adults that don't fit into discrete disease categories but significantly impact health and quality of life.
- **Priority Facts**: Includes risk factors like polypharmacy, muscle weakness, cognitive impairment, and environmental hazards.
- **NCLEX Pearls**: Implement preventive strategies and tailored interventions.
- **Top Safety Tips**: Assess home safety for fall risks, monitor cognitive status, and address underlying causes of incontinence.
- **Sample Question**: What is a key nursing action to prevent falls in older adults?
- A. Restricting the patient's mobility to reduce fall risk.
- B. Conducting regular assessments for fall risk factors and modifying the environment accordingly.
- C. Advising the use of sedatives to prevent wandering.
- D. Ignoring minor falls if there are no immediate injuries.
- **Correct Answer**: B. Conducting regular assessments for fall risk factors and modifying the environment accordingly.
- **Rationale**: Regular assessment of fall risk factors and environmental modifications are critical in preventing falls in older adults, enhancing safety, and maintaining mobility.

Dementia and Alzheimer's Disease

- **Description**: Progressive neurological disorders affecting memory, thinking, behavior, and the ability to perform everyday activities.
- **Priority Facts**: Alzheimer's is the most common form of dementia.
- **NCLEX Pearls**: Focus on maintaining patient dignity, supporting functional abilities, and managing behavioral changes.
- **Top Safety Tips**: Ensure a safe environment, use simple and clear communication, and involve caregivers in care planning.

- **Sample Question**: What is essential in the care of a patient with Alzheimer's disease?
- A. Using complex explanations to keep the brain active.
- B. Maintaining routine and familiarity to minimize confusion and agitation.
- C. Isolating the patient to prevent overstimulation.
- D. Frequently changing care providers to introduce variety.
- **Correct Answer**: B. Maintaining routine and familiarity to minimize confusion and agitation.
- **Rationale**: Consistent routines and familiar environments help reduce confusion and agitation in patients with Alzheimer's disease, providing a sense of security and stability.

Medication Management in Older Adults

- **Description**: Optimizing medication use to improve health outcomes in the elderly, considering the challenges of polypharmacy and age-related physiological changes.
- **Priority Facts**: Older adults are more susceptible to adverse drug reactions due to factors like renal function decline and drug interactions.
- **NCLEX Pearls**: Regularly review medications for necessity and potential interactions.
- **Top Safety Tips**: Educate on the correct use of medications, monitor for side effects, and simplify regimens where possible.
- **Sample Question**: What is a priority consideration in medication management for older adults?
- A. Automatically discontinuing all non-essential medications without consulting the healthcare provider.
- B. Regular medication review to assess for efficacy, side effects, and interactions.
- C. Prescribing the highest dose initially to achieve quick therapeutic effects.
- D. Assuming older adults will report all side effects without prompting.

- **Correct Answer**: B. Regular medication review to assess for efficacy, side effects, and interactions.
- **Rationale**: Regular reviews of medication in older adults are crucial to ensure that each medication is still necessary, effective, and not causing adverse interactions, considering the increased risk of side effects and interactions in this population.

End-of-Life and Palliative Care in Geriatrics

- **Description**: Care focused on providing comfort and quality of life for older adults approaching the end of life, including pain management and emotional support.
- **Priority Facts**: Involves managing symptoms, addressing psychological and spiritual needs, and supporting the family.
- **NCLEX Pearls**: Understand the physical and emotional aspects of end-of-life care; communicate sensitively about death and dying.
- **Top Safety Tips**: Regularly assess pain and discomfort, provide appropriate symptom management, and respect patient and family wishes.
- **Sample Question**: What is a key nursing action in providing palliative care to an elderly patient?
- A. Avoiding discussions about death to prevent distress.
- B. Focusing solely on aggressive curative treatments.
- C. Providing comprehensive symptom management and emotional support.
- D. Limiting family visits to reduce patient fatigue.
- **Correct Answer**: C. Providing comprehensive symptom management and emotional support.
- **Rationale**: Palliative care involves comprehensive management of physical symptoms and providing emotional and spiritual support to both the patient and their family.

Long-Term Care and Rehabilitation

- **Description**: Provision of medical, nursing, and rehabilitative care to individuals who require assistance with daily living due to chronic health conditions or disabilities.
- **Priority Facts**: Includes a multidisciplinary approach to care, focusing on maintaining functional abilities and quality of life.
- **NCLEX Pearls**: Tailor care plans to individual needs; coordinate with various healthcare professionals.
- **Top Safety Tips**: Monitor for changes in health status, prevent complications like pressure ulcers and infections, and ensure a safe environment.
- **Sample Question**: What is essential in the management of a patient in long-term care?
- A. Keeping the patient bedridden to prevent falls.
- B. Encouraging independence in activities of daily living as much as possible.
- C. Focusing care exclusively on physical health, neglecting mental well-being.
- D. Changing care routines frequently to keep the environment stimulating.
- **Correct Answer**: B. Encouraging independence in activities of daily living as much as possible.
- **Rationale**: Promoting independence in daily activities is key in long-term care to maintain the patient's functional ability and dignity.

Elder Abuse and Neglect

- **Description**: Recognition and management of physical, emotional, or financial abuse or neglect of older adults.
- **Priority Facts**: Includes identifying signs of abuse or neglect, such as unexplained injuries, withdrawal, or financial discrepancies.
- **NCLEX Pearls**: Be vigilant for signs of abuse, understand mandatory reporting laws, and provide a safe environment.

- **Top Safety Tips**: Document concerns thoroughly, report suspicions according to protocol, and provide support to the victim.
- **Sample Question**: What is a nurse's responsibility if elder abuse is suspected?
- A. Confront the suspected abuser directly.
- B. Wait for concrete proof before reporting.
- C. Report the suspicion to appropriate authorities as required by law.
- D. Discuss suspicions with other patients to gather more information.
- **Correct Answer**: C. Report the suspicion to appropriate authorities as required by law.
- **Rationale**: Mandatory reporting laws require healthcare professionals to report any suspicions of elder abuse to protect the victim and ensure their safety.

Aging and Mental Health

- **Description**: Addressing mental health issues in older adults, including depression, anxiety, and cognitive changes associated with aging.
- **Priority Facts**: Mental health issues in older adults may be underdiagnosed or misattributed to aging.
- **NCLEX Pearls**: Screen for mental health issues, provide appropriate interventions, and consider the impact of comorbidities.
- **Top Safety Tips**: Monitor for medication side effects, offer supportive therapy, and engage family or caregivers in care when appropriate.
- **Sample Question**: What is important to consider in managing mental health in older adults?
- A. Assuming that cognitive decline is an inevitable part of aging.
- B. Regularly screening for mental health issues and tailoring interventions to the individual.
- C. Focusing only on pharmacological interventions for all mental health issues.
- D. Dismissing symptoms of depression as normal reactions to aging.
- **Correct Answer**: B. Regularly screening for mental health issues and

tailoring interventions to the individual.
- **Rationale**: Regular screening and individualized interventions are crucial in managing mental health in older adults, as symptoms may be overlooked or attributed solely to aging.

Chronic Disease Management in Older Adults

- **Description**: Coordinated care approach to manage chronic diseases like diabetes, heart disease, and arthritis in older adults.
- **Priority Facts**: Involves medication management, lifestyle modifications, and monitoring for complications.
- **NCLEX Pearls**: Understand the complexities of managing multiple chronic conditions.
- **Top Safety Tips**: Educate about disease management, ensure adherence to treatment plans, and coordinate care with other health professionals.
- **Sample Question**: What is a key aspect of managing chronic disease in older adults?
- A. Reliance on family members to make all healthcare decisions.
- B. Comprehensive management addressing both physical and psychosocial needs.
- C. Using only alternative therapies to avoid side effects of medications.
- D. Simplifying the regimen by discontinuing most medications.
- **Correct Answer**: B. Comprehensive management addressing both physical and psychosocial needs.
- **Rationale**: Managing chronic disease in older adults requires a comprehensive approach that addresses physical, emotional, and social aspects, ensuring holistic care.

Nutrition and Hydration in the Elderly

- **Description**: Ensuring adequate nutrition and hydration in older adults, addressing challenges like decreased appetite, difficulty swallowing, and changes in metabolism.

- **Priority Facts**: Poor nutrition and dehydration can exacerbate chronic conditions and impact recovery.
- **NCLEX Pearls**: Monitor dietary intake, identify potential barriers to good nutrition, and adapt diets to specific needs and preferences.
- **Top Safety Tips**: Assess for signs of malnutrition and dehydration, encourage regular fluid intake, and coordinate with dietitians for tailored meal plans.
- **Sample Question**: What is a key consideration for ensuring proper nutrition in an elderly patient?
- A. Applying the same nutritional guidelines used for younger adults.
- B. Encouraging large, less frequent meals to reduce preparation effort.
- C. Assessing ability to eat independently and modifying diets as needed.
- D. Avoiding fluids to reduce the risk of incontinence.
- **Correct Answer**: C. Assessing ability to eat independently and modifying diets as needed.
- **Rationale**: Assessing the ability to eat independently and modifying diets are crucial in the elderly to address issues like difficulty swallowing or decreased appetite, ensuring adequate nutrition and hydration.

Mobility and Safety Issues in Geriatrics

- **Description**: Addressing the challenges older adults face with mobility, including the risk of falls, and implementing strategies to improve safety.
- **Priority Facts**: Mobility issues can lead to falls, reduced independence, and decreased quality of life.
- **NCLEX Pearls**: Regularly assess mobility, strength, and balance; understand the impact of medications on fall risk.
- **Top Safety Tips**: Implement fall prevention strategies, encourage safe exercise, and modify the environment for safety.
- **Sample Question**: What is an essential strategy in preventing falls in elderly patients?
- A. Restricting all physical activity to reduce the risk of falls.
- B. Using restraints whenever the patient is left unattended.

- C. Ensuring the environment is safe and free from hazards.
- D. Ignoring minor trips and slips if no injury occurs.
- **Correct Answer**: C. Ensuring the environment is safe and free from hazards.
- **Rationale**: A safe environment, free from hazards, is key in preventing falls in the elderly. This includes adequate lighting, removing tripping hazards, and installing grab bars in necessary areas.

9

Community and Public Health Nursing

Epidemiology and Disease Surveillance

- **Description**: The study of the distribution and determinants of health-related states or events in specified populations, and the application of this study to control health problems.
- **Priority Facts**: Includes tracking the spread of diseases, identifying risk factors, and informing public health policies.
- **NCLEX Pearls**: Understand common epidemiological terms and concepts; recognize the significance of disease surveillance in public health.
- **Top Safety Tips**: Stay informed about current epidemiological data, report notifiable diseases promptly, and participate in surveillance activities.
- **Sample Question**: Why is disease surveillance important in public health nursing?
- A. To provide individualized care to each patient.
- B. For early detection and control of outbreaks to prevent widespread transmission.
- C. To limit healthcare interventions to only those with high-risk factors.
- D. For the purpose of medical research only.
- **Correct Answer**: B. For early detection and control of outbreaks to prevent

widespread transmission.
- **Rationale**: Disease surveillance is crucial for the early detection and control of outbreaks, allowing for timely interventions to prevent and reduce the spread of diseases.

Community Health Assessment and Planning

- **Description**: A systematic examination of the health status indicators for a given population that is used to identify key issues and assets in a community.
- **Priority Facts**: Involves data collection, analysis, and collaboration with community stakeholders.
- **NCLEX Pearls**: Recognize the importance of community involvement in health assessment and planning.
- **Top Safety Tips**: Ensure inclusivity in assessment processes; base interventions on evidence-based practices.
- **Sample Question**: What is a critical step in community health assessment and planning?
- A. Implementing programs without community input for efficiency.
- B. Engaging the community in identifying health needs and resources.
- C. Focusing solely on a single health issue disregarding others.
- D. Assuming healthcare professionals understand the community needs without assessment.
- **Correct Answer**: B. Engaging the community in identifying health needs and resources.
- **Rationale**: Active community engagement is essential in identifying specific health needs and resources, ensuring that health plans are relevant and effective.

Health Promotion and Disease Prevention Programs

- **Description**: Initiatives designed to enhance health and prevent disease, such as vaccination programs, lifestyle education, and screening initiatives.
- **Priority Facts**: Target specific populations and focus on reducing risk factors.
- **NCLEX Pearls**: Understand different levels of disease prevention (primary, secondary, tertiary); advocate for evidence-based health promotion activities.
- **Top Safety Tips**: Educate the public on health promotion, provide culturally appropriate health information, and support accessibility to prevention programs.
- **Sample Question**: What is a fundamental aspect of health promotion and disease prevention programs?
- A. Focusing only on high-cost interventions for maximum profit.
- B. Providing education and resources to support healthy lifestyle choices and disease prevention.
- C. Limiting access to preventive services to decrease healthcare spending.
- D. Promoting health initiatives only in high-income areas.
- **Correct Answer**: B. Providing education and resources to support healthy lifestyle choices and disease prevention.
- **Rationale**: Fundamental to these programs is providing education and resources that empower individuals and communities to make informed choices about their health, thereby preventing disease and promoting wellness.

Global Health and Emerging Diseases

- **Description**: Addressing health issues that transcend national boundaries, focusing on emerging diseases and international health initiatives.
- **Priority Facts**: Involves understanding the global burden of disease, international health regulations, and strategies for disease control.

- **NCLEX Pearls**: Stay informed about global health trends and emerging diseases; understand the role of international health organizations.
- **Top Safety Tips**: Advocate for global vaccination efforts, promote awareness of emerging diseases, and support measures to prevent global disease transmission.
- **Sample Question**: Why is an understanding of global health important for nurses?
- A. To limit nursing care to local communities only.
- B. Because health issues in one part of the world can impact health globally.
- C. To focus solely on diseases prevalent in the nurse's own country.
- D. Global health is irrelevant to nursing practice.
- **Correct Answer**: B. Because health issues in one part of the world can impact health globally.
- **Rationale**: Global health is important as diseases and health issues can quickly cross borders, making an understanding of global health trends and issues essential for effective healthcare delivery and disease prevention.

Environmental and Occupational Health

- **Description**: Focus on the impact of environmental and occupational factors on health and the implementation of strategies to reduce associated risks.
- **Priority Facts**: Includes workplace safety, exposure to environmental toxins, and the impact of environmental conditions on health.
- **NCLEX Pearls**: Recognize the influence of environmental and occupational factors on health; promote safe work practices.
- **Top Safety Tips**: Educate about minimizing exposure to environmental hazards; advocate for policies promoting environmental and occupational health.
- **Sample Question**: What is an essential component of environmental and occupational health in nursing?

- A. Ignoring environmental risks as they are outside the scope of nursing.
- B. Educating about and advocating for safe and healthy environments.
- C. Focusing only on individual health behaviors, not environmental factors.
- D. Leaving environmental health concerns to environmental scientists.
- **Correct Answer**: B. Educating about and advocating for safe and healthy environments.
- **Rationale**: A key component is educating about environmental and occupational risks and advocating for changes to promote safe and healthy environments.

Disaster Preparedness and Response

- **Description**: Activities and protocols established to prepare for, respond to, and recover from disasters, both natural and man-made.
- **Priority Facts**: Involves risk assessment, resource management, and coordination with emergency services.
- **NCLEX Pearls**: Be familiar with local disaster response plans; understand the nurse's role in different phases of disaster management.
- **Top Safety Tips**: Participate in disaster drills, maintain personal preparedness, and educate the community on disaster response.
- **Sample Question**: What is the MOST important action for a nurse during disaster response?
- A. Waiting for external aid before taking any action.
- B. Immediately providing care independently without coordination.
- C. Engaging in disaster response activities based on established protocols and training.
- D. Focusing solely on physical injuries, ignoring psychological impacts.
- **Correct Answer**: C. Engaging in disaster response activities based on established protocols and training.
- **Rationale**: Following established protocols and training is crucial in disaster response to ensure effective, coordinated care and resource utilization.

Health Education and Community Outreach

- **Description**: Providing information and resources to individuals and communities to promote health and prevent illness.
- **Priority Facts**: Includes topics like nutrition, physical activity, chronic disease management, and preventive health screenings.
- **NCLEX Pearls**: Use culturally appropriate methods to educate; involve community leaders in outreach programs.
- **Top Safety Tips**: Communicate in a language and manner understandable to the community; consider literacy levels and cultural norms.
- **Sample Question**: What is a key element of effective health education and community outreach?
- A. Using medical jargon to establish authority.
- B. Delivering standardized messages without adapting to specific community needs.
- C. Tailoring health messages to meet the unique needs of the community.
- D. Limiting outreach efforts to high-income populations.
- **Correct Answer**: C. Tailoring health messages to meet the unique needs of the community.
- **Rationale**: Adapting health education to the specific needs of the community ensures relevance, effectiveness, and higher engagement in health promotion activities.

School Health Nursing

- **Description**: Provision of health services, education, and counseling in a school setting to promote the well-being of students.
- **Priority Facts**: Involves managing acute and chronic health issues, health education, and supporting students with special healthcare needs.
- **NCLEX Pearls**: Collaborate with educators, parents, and students; understand developmental stages and school policies.
- **Top Safety Tips**: Monitor for signs of abuse or developmental issues; manage medications and emergencies effectively.

- **Sample Question**: What is an essential role of a school nurse?
- A. Exclusively treating injuries and illnesses that occur at school.
- B. Providing comprehensive health services, including health education and managing chronic conditions in students.
- C. Delegating all health-related responsibilities to teachers.
- D. Focusing only on health issues reported by parents.
- **Correct Answer**: B. Providing comprehensive health services, including health education and managing chronic conditions in students.
- **Rationale**: The school nurse plays a multifaceted role, not only treating injuries and illnesses but also managing chronic health conditions, providing health education, and addressing broader health needs of students.

Home Health Nursing

- **Description**: Nursing care provided in a patient's home, focusing on maintaining and restoring health or managing chronic illness.
- **Priority Facts**: Includes post-operative care, chronic disease management, wound care, and elderly care.
- **NCLEX Pearls**: Adapt care plans to the home environment; involve and educate family caregivers.
- **Top Safety Tips**: Assess the safety of the home environment; manage medications and equipment effectively.
- **Sample Question**: What is crucial for effective home health nursing?
- A. Providing care without family involvement to simplify processes.
- B. Developing individualized care plans that consider the patient's home environment and caregiver resources.
- C. Limiting visits to reduce healthcare costs, regardless of patient needs.
- D. Only addressing acute medical issues, neglecting long-term care needs.
- **Correct Answer**: B. Developing individualized care plans that consider the patient's home environment and caregiver resources.
- **Rationale**: Individualized care plans that consider the unique aspects of

the home environment and available resources are essential for effective home health nursing, ensuring patient needs are met comprehensively.

Public Health Policy and Advocacy

- **Description**: Involvement in the development and implementation of health policies, advocating for public health improvements and equity.
- **Priority Facts**: Nurses play a key role in shaping health policy, based on their expertise and frontline experience.
- **NCLEX Pearls**: Understand the policy-making process; advocate for policies that improve health outcomes and access to care.
- **Top Safety Tips**: Engage in evidence-based advocacy; stay informed about current public health issues and policies.
- **Sample Question**: Why is public health policy and advocacy important in nursing?
- A. To focus nursing care solely on individual patient advocacy.
- B. Engaging in policy development and advocacy to improve health care for all populations, particularly the underserved.
- C. To prioritize healthcare policies that benefit healthcare providers over patients.
- D. To remove nurses from direct patient care and focus exclusively on policy.
- **Correct Answer**: B. Engaging in policy development and advocacy to improve health care for all populations, particularly the underserved.
- **Rationale**: Nurses' involvement in policy and advocacy is crucial to leveraging their expertise and insights to shape health policies that improve care quality and access, particularly for underserved communities.

Vulnerable Populations and Access to Care

- **Description**: Focus on groups who have limited resources and access to healthcare, such as the homeless, low-income families, and certain ethnic minorities.

- **Priority Facts**: These populations face barriers like financial constraints, lack of insurance, and geographic isolation.
- **NCLEX Pearls**: Understand social determinants of health; advocate for equitable access to healthcare services.
- **Top Safety Tips**: Tailor care plans to address specific barriers; connect patients with community resources and support programs.
- **Sample Question**: What is an important consideration when providing care to vulnerable populations?
- A. Providing the same level of care as for non-vulnerable populations without adaptations.
- B. Identifying and addressing barriers to healthcare access and adherence to treatment plans.
- C. Assuming all individuals in vulnerable populations have the same healthcare needs.
- D. Focusing exclusively on immediate medical needs, ignoring social and environmental factors.
- **Correct Answer**: B. Identifying and addressing barriers to healthcare access and adherence to treatment plans.
- **Rationale**: Understanding and addressing the unique barriers faced by vulnerable populations are crucial for ensuring effective and equitable healthcare access and improving health outcomes.

Cultural Competence and Health Literacy

- **Description**: The ability of healthcare providers to understand and effectively respond to the cultural and language needs of patients from diverse backgrounds.
- **Priority Facts**: Involves awareness of cultural differences, effective communication, and respect for patient values and beliefs.
- **NCLEX Pearls**: Engage in active listening, avoid making assumptions based on stereotypes, and use culturally sensitive communication strategies.
- **Top Safety Tips**: Use language services when needed, provide health ed-

ucation in understandable formats, and respect cultural health practices.
- **Sample Question**: Why is cultural competence important in nursing care?
- A. To apply a uniform approach to care regardless of cultural background.
- B. To better understand and meet the diverse needs of patients, improving health outcomes.
- C. To focus only on the cultural aspects of care while ignoring medical evidence.
- D. To prioritize cultural practices over established medical protocols.
- **Correct Answer**: B. To better understand and meet the diverse needs of patients, improving health outcomes.
- **Rationale**: Cultural competence enables nurses to understand and respect the diverse backgrounds and needs of patients, leading to more effective communication, increased patient trust, and improved health outcomes.

10

Leadership and Management in Nursing

Nursing Leadership Styles and Theories

- **Description**: Various approaches to leadership within nursing, including transformational, transactional, and democratic styles.
- **Priority Facts**: Effective leadership styles in nursing can impact patient care outcomes and staff satisfaction.
- **NCLEX Pearls**: Understand the impact of different leadership styles on team dynamics and patient care.
- **Top Safety Tips**: Adopt a leadership style that promotes a safe, efficient, and collaborative work environment.
- **Sample Question**: Why is understanding different leadership styles important for a nurse leader?
- A. To adopt a single style for all situations.
- B. To apply the most authoritative style in all scenarios.
- C. To tailor leadership approach based on team needs and patient care situations.
- D. To avoid taking on any leadership responsibilities.
- **Correct Answer**: C. To tailor leadership approach based on team needs and patient care situations.
- **Rationale**: Flexibility in leadership style allows nurse leaders to adapt

to varying team dynamics and patient care scenarios, promoting more effective management and better care outcomes.

Team Building and Interprofessional Collaboration

- **Description**: Strategies for creating and maintaining effective teamwork among healthcare professionals from various disciplines.
- **Priority Facts**: Effective team building enhances communication, collaboration, and patient care outcomes.
- **NCLEX Pearls**: Promote open communication and respect for diverse roles and expertise in healthcare teams.
- **Top Safety Tips**: Foster a team culture where safety concerns can be freely discussed and addressed.
- **Sample Question**: What is an essential component of successful team building and interprofessional collaboration?
- A. Encouraging competition among team members to improve performance.
- B. Fostering an environment of mutual respect and open communication.
- C. Having one discipline dominate the decision-making process.
- D. Isolating team issues from management to avoid conflict.
- **Correct Answer**: B. Fostering an environment of mutual respect and open communication.
- **Rationale**: Creating an atmosphere of mutual respect and open communication is key in effective team building and interprofessional collaboration, leading to improved patient care and work satisfaction.

Conflict Resolution and Negotiation

- **Description**: Approaches and techniques used to resolve disagreements and conflicts in a professional and constructive manner.
- **Priority Facts**: Conflict resolution skills are essential for maintaining a harmonious and productive work environment.
- **NCLEX Pearls**: Utilize active listening, empathy, and clear communica-

tion to resolve conflicts.
- **Top Safety Tips**: Address conflicts promptly to prevent escalation and impact on patient care.
- **Sample Question**: What is a critical skill for nurses in conflict resolution?
- A. Avoiding any conflicts to maintain a superficial appearance of harmony.
- B. Addressing conflicts directly and seeking mutually acceptable solutions.
- C. Allowing conflicts to resolve naturally without intervention.
- D. Resorting to higher authorities for all types of conflicts.
- **Correct Answer**: B. Addressing conflicts directly and seeking mutually acceptable solutions.
- **Rationale**: Directly addressing conflicts and working towards mutually acceptable solutions is essential to maintain a functional and collaborative work environment.

Quality Improvement and Patient Safety

- **Description**: Continuous efforts to improve the quality of healthcare delivery and ensure patient safety.
- **Priority Facts**: Involves analyzing performance, implementing improvements, and monitoring outcomes.
- **NCLEX Pearls**: Be proactive in identifying areas for improvement and engage in evidence-based practices to enhance patient safety.
- **Top Safety Tips**: Regularly review and update protocols to reflect best practices; encourage a culture of safety.
- **Sample Question**: What is an essential aspect of quality improvement in nursing?
- A. Focusing solely on individual performance, ignoring systemic issues.
- B. Implementing changes without evaluating their impact on patient outcomes.
- C. Involving frontline staff in identifying problems and developing solutions.

- D. Assuming that current practices are always the best practices.
- **Correct Answer**: C. Involving frontline staff in identifying problems and developing solutions.
- **Rationale**: Involvement of frontline staff in the quality improvement process is crucial as they are often the first to identify areas for improvement and can provide practical, patient-centered solutions.

Evidence-Based Practice and Research Utilization

- **Description**: Integration of the best current research evidence with clinical expertise and patient values in the decision-making process for patient care.
- **Priority Facts**: Evidence-based practice improves patient outcomes and contributes to healthcare quality.
- **NCLEX Pearls**: Stay informed about the latest research and guidelines; critically appraise evidence for its applicability to patient care.
- **Top Safety Tips**: Apply research findings appropriately in practice; ensure interventions are based on sound evidence.
- **Sample Question**: Why is evidence-based practice important in nursing?
- A. To rely exclusively on historical practices without considering current evidence.
- B. To implement new interventions based solely on personal preference.
- C. To integrate the best current evidence with clinical expertise for optimal patient care.
- D. To disregard patient preferences in favor of research findings.
- **Correct Answer**: C. To integrate the best current evidence with clinical expertise for optimal patient care.
- **Rationale**: Evidence-based practice involves combining the best available research, clinical expertise, and patient values to provide high-quality, patient-centered care.

Healthcare Policy and Regulation

- **Description**: The creation and implementation of policies and laws that govern the operation of healthcare systems and the delivery of care.
- **Priority Facts**: Involves understanding healthcare laws, accreditation standards, and regulatory requirements.
- **NCLEX Pearls**: Nurses need to be aware of healthcare policies and regulations affecting their practice and patient care.
- **Top Safety Tips**: Adhere to legal and regulatory standards in all aspects of patient care.
- **Sample Question**: What is an essential aspect of healthcare policy and regulation for nurses?
- A. Ignoring policy changes as they are irrelevant to daily nursing practice.
- B. Regularly updating knowledge on healthcare policies and regulatory changes.
- C. Focusing only on clinical skills, leaving policy understanding to administrators.
- D. Adhering strictly to old policies, regardless of updates or changes.
- **Correct Answer**: B. Regularly updating knowledge on healthcare policies and regulatory changes.
- **Rationale**: Staying informed about current healthcare policies and regulations is crucial for nurses to ensure compliance and provide safe, legal, and effective patient care.

Staff Development and Training

- **Description**: Activities and programs aimed at enhancing the skills, knowledge, and competencies of healthcare staff.
- **Priority Facts**: Continuous staff development improves patient care quality and workplace efficiency.
- **NCLEX Pearls**: Encourage lifelong learning and participation in professional development opportunities.
- **Top Safety Tips**: Provide training in the latest patient care techniques

and technology.
- **Sample Question**: Why is ongoing staff development and training important in nursing?
- A. To reduce the workload of senior staff.
- B. To ensure that staff remain updated on current best practices and technologies.
- C. To focus only on theoretical knowledge, disregarding practical skills.
- D. To limit training to new staff members only.
- **Correct Answer**: B. To ensure that staff remain updated on current best practices and technologies.
- **Rationale**: Ongoing staff development and training are crucial for keeping nurses updated on the latest best practices, technologies, and skills, which is essential for delivering high-quality patient care.

Ethical Decision Making in Leadership

- **Description**: The process of making choices that align with ethical standards and values in leadership roles.
- **Priority Facts**: Involves balancing competing interests and values, maintaining integrity, and prioritizing patient welfare.
- **NCLEX Pearls**: Utilize ethical frameworks and principles when making decisions affecting staff and patients.
- **Top Safety Tips**: Make decisions that promote patient safety and uphold ethical standards.
- **Sample Question**: What is key to ethical decision making in nursing leadership?
- A. Basing all decisions on financial considerations.
- B. Following ethical principles to guide decision-making processes.
- C. Making decisions unilaterally without consulting relevant stakeholders.
- D. Prioritizing administrative convenience over patient needs.
- **Correct Answer**: B. Following ethical principles to guide decision-making processes.

- **Rationale**: Ethical decision making in nursing leadership requires adhering to ethical principles, ensuring decisions are made fairly, responsibly, and with a focus on patient welfare.

Resource Management and Budgeting

- **Description**: Efficient and effective allocation and use of resources, including staff, supplies, and finances.
- **Priority Facts**: Effective resource management is crucial for maintaining the quality of care while controlling costs.
- **NCLEX Pearls**: Understand basic budgeting and resource allocation principles; advocate for resources necessary for quality patient care.
- **Top Safety Tips**: Use resources wisely to ensure patient safety and care quality are not compromised.
- **Sample Question**: Why is resource management and budgeting important in nursing?
- A. To allocate resources indiscriminately without considering patient needs.
- B. To ensure that necessary resources are available for optimal patient care.
- C. To cut costs in all areas, regardless of the impact on patient care.
- D. To centralize all decision-making regarding resources at the administrative level.
- **Correct Answer**: B. To ensure that necessary resources are available for optimal patient care.
- **Rationale**: Effective resource management and budgeting are crucial in nursing to ensure the necessary resources are available and used efficiently, thereby maintaining high standards of patient care.

Health Informatics and Technology in Nursing

- **Description**: The use of information technology and data management systems to improve healthcare delivery and patient outcomes.
- **Priority Facts**: Involves electronic health records, telehealth, data analysis, and information security.
- **NCLEX Pearls**: Stay current with emerging technologies and informatics trends that impact nursing practice.
- **Top Safety Tips**: Safeguard patient data, and use technology to enhance, not replace, the nurse-patient relationship.
- **Sample Question**: What is the role of health informatics and technology in nursing?
- A. Avoiding all forms of technology in patient care.
- B. Utilizing technology and informatics to improve patient care and enhance clinical practices.
- C. Completely replacing traditional nursing methods with technology-based solutions.
- D. Focusing solely on technology, disregarding the importance of direct patient care.
- **Correct Answer**: B. Utilizing technology and informatics to improve patient care and enhance clinical practices.
- **Rationale**: Health informatics and technology play a significant role in modern nursing by improving the efficiency and effectiveness of patient care through better data management, patient monitoring, and information access.

Organizational Change and Innovation

- **Description**: The process of implementing new ideas, methods, and strategies in healthcare settings to improve efficiency, patient care, and outcomes.
- **Priority Facts**: Involves understanding the need for change, managing resistance, and effectively communicating change.

- **NCLEX Pearls**: Embrace change as a constant in healthcare; understand the theories and models of change management.
- **Top Safety Tips**: Ensure changes do not compromise patient safety; involve staff at all levels in the change process for smooth implementation.
- **Sample Question**: What is a crucial factor for a nurse leader to consider during organizational change?
- A. Implementing changes rapidly without seeking staff input.
- B. Maintaining the status quo regardless of external pressures.
- C. Engaging and communicating effectively with staff throughout the change process.
- D. Overlooking the impact of changes on patient care and staff workload.
- **Correct Answer**: C. Engaging and communicating effectively with staff throughout the change process.
- **Rationale**: Effective engagement and communication with staff are key to successfully managing organizational change. It helps in understanding the impact of changes, addressing concerns, and ensuring a collaborative approach for successful implementation.

11

Comprehensive Test Preparation

NCLEX-RN Exam Structure and Format

- As you prepare to take the NCLEX-RN exam, understanding its structure and format is crucial for success.
- **Familiarize with the CAT Format**: The NCLEX-RN uses Computerized Adaptive Testing (CAT). This means that the difficulty of the questions adapts based on your answers. Start with understanding how CAT works, as this will help you manage your expectations during the exam.
- **Know the Question Types**: The exam includes a variety of question formats such as multiple-choice, select-all-that-apply (SATA), hot spots, fill-in-the-blank, and ordered response. Familiarize yourself with these formats, as practicing different types will boost your confidence.
- **Understand the Length and Timing**: The exam can range from 75 to 265 questions and you have up to 6 hours to complete it. This includes optional breaks. Time management is key, so practice pacing yourself during mock exams.
- **Study the Test Plan**: The National Council of State Boards of Nursing (NCSBN) provides a test plan outlining the content areas covered. These include Safe and Effective Care Environment, Health Promotion and Maintenance, Psychosocial Integrity, and Physiological Integrity. Review

this plan thoroughly to understand the distribution of questions.
- **Practice with NCLEX-Style Questions**: Engage with as many practice questions as possible. This will not only familiarize you with the style and complexity of the questions but also helps in identifying areas where you need more review.
- **Simulate Exam Conditions**: While studying, try to simulate exam conditions. This includes timing yourself, taking breaks as you would during the actual exam, and creating an environment similar to a test center.
- **Prepare for Variable Length**: Since the exam uses the CAT format, it ends when it determines with 95% confidence that your performance is either above or below the passing standard. Prepare mentally for the exam to end at any time after the minimum number of questions.
- **Review the Basics**: Don't overlook the basics. Make sure you're clear on fundamental nursing concepts, as these are the foundation upon which more complex questions are built.
- **Focus on Critical Thinking and Application**: The NCLEX-RN tests your ability to apply knowledge in real-life scenarios. Enhance your critical thinking skills by practicing with scenario-based questions.
- **Stay Calm and Positive**: Lastly, maintaining a positive attitude and staying calm are essential. Remember, the exam is designed to determine your readiness for entry-level nursing, not to trick you.

Test-Taking Strategies and Tips

- Taking the NCLEX-RN can be a daunting experience, but with the right strategies and mindset, you can approach it with confidence.
- **Understand the Question Before Answering**: Carefully read each question and understand what it's asking. Pay attention to words like "first," "best," "most," or "initial," as they can significantly alter the meaning of the question.
- **Don't Rush, but Be Conscious of Time**: While it's important not to rush through the questions, being aware of the time is crucial. If you find

yourself spending too long on a question, it might be best to make your best guess and move on.
- **Eliminate Obviously Wrong Answers**: In multiple-choice questions, start by eliminating the choices that are clearly incorrect. This increases your chances if you need to make an educated guess.
- **Look for Keywords**: Keywords in a question can provide clues about the correct answer. Words that indicate urgency (e.g., acute, severe, immediate) might suggest prioritizing certain actions.
- **Trust Your First Instinct**: Often, your first answer choice is likely to be correct unless you realize you misread the question. Avoid changing your answers unless you have a strong reason.
- **Use the Process of Elimination**: For more difficult questions, use the process of elimination to narrow down your choices. Even if you're unsure, eliminating one or two choices can significantly improve your odds.
- **Beware of Absolutes**: Be cautious with answer choices that use absolute terms like "always" or "never." In healthcare, there are few absolutes, and such options may be incorrect.
- **Prioritize Patient Safety and Needs**: When in doubt, choose the option that prioritizes patient safety and meets immediate patient needs, especially in prioritization questions.
- **Stay Calm and Take Deep Breaths**: If you feel overwhelmed, take a moment to breathe deeply. Panic can cloud your judgment, so staying calm is key.
- **Plan for Breaks**: You have up to 6 hours to complete the exam, with optional breaks. Plan to use these breaks to refresh yourself, especially if you feel fatigued.
- **Review Lab Values and Medications**: Be familiar with common lab values and medications, as these often feature in NCLEX-RN questions.
- **Practice with NCLEX-Style Questions**: Regular practice with NCLEX-style questions can help you get used to the format and the kind of critical thinking the exam requires.
- **Don't Overlook the Simple Answer**: Sometimes the simplest answer

is the correct one. Don't overthink and complicate the question if a straightforward answer seems to fit.
- **Prepare Mentally for the Exam Length**: The exam can end anytime after the minimum 75 questions, so be mentally prepared for both a shorter and a longer test.

Prioritization and Delegation Questions

- Tackling prioritization and delegation questions in the NCLEX-RN can be challenging, but they are crucial for assessing your ability to manage real-world nursing scenarios.
- **Understand the Hierarchy of Needs**: Familiarize yourself with Maslow's Hierarchy of Needs. In prioritization questions, patient needs related to physiological and safety concerns usually take precedence.
- **Recognize Urgent Situations**: Identify which patient scenarios describe the most urgent situations. Questions may present multiple patients, but your job is to determine who needs immediate attention based on the severity of their condition.
- **Use ABCs as a Guide**: Remember the ABCs (Airway, Breathing, Circulation) as a priority-setting framework. Issues affecting a patient's airway, breathing, or circulation are generally the most urgent.
- **Identify Stable vs. Unstable Patients**: Prioritize care for unstable patients over stable ones. Signs of instability can include abnormal vital signs, acute pain, or altered mental status.
- **Understand Scope of Practice**: For delegation questions, know the scope of practice and competencies of different team members (e.g., RNs, LPNs, CNAs). Delegate tasks appropriately based on each team member's qualifications.
- **Never Delegate Assessment, Planning, Evaluation**: Remember that as an RN, you should never delegate assessment, planning, evaluation, or any task requiring nursing judgment to LPNs or CNAs.
- **Consider Patient Safety and Infection Control**: Prioritize actions that

ensure patient safety and adhere to infection control standards.
- **Evaluate Task Urgency and Complexity**: Delegate tasks that are routine and non-complex, while retaining more complex care responsibilities.
- **Use Critical Thinking**: Apply your clinical judgment and critical thinking skills to determine the best course of action in each scenario.
- **Practice with Scenario-Based Questions**: The more you practice with NCLEX-style prioritization and delegation questions, the more confident you'll become in your decision-making skills.
- **Review Policies and Best Practices**: Be familiar with general nursing policies and best practices, as they often guide prioritization and delegation decisions.
- **Don't Forget to Follow Up**: Remember, delegation isn't just about assigning tasks. It's also about ensuring the task was completed correctly and safely.
- **Stay Updated with Guidelines**: Keep abreast of current guidelines and protocols, as these can influence priority decisions, especially in emergent situations.
- **Prioritize Communication**: Effective communication is key in delegation. Ensure instructions are clear and concise.

Select All That Apply (SATA) Question Strategies

- Select All That Apply (SATA) questions can be one of the more challenging aspects of the NCLEX-RN exam, as they require a deep understanding of the topic and the ability to discern subtle nuances in options.
- **Treat Each Option as a True/False Question**: Consider each option independently and determine if it's true or false. This can make the process less overwhelming and help you focus on each statement's validity.
- **Don't Look for a Pattern**: There's no standard number of correct answers in SATA questions. Avoid trying to guess the number of correct options and focus on the content instead.
- **Understand the Question Completely**: Before looking at the options,

ensure you fully understand what the question is asking. Misinterpreting the question can lead to incorrect answers.
- **Use Elimination Tactics**: If you're certain an option is incorrect, eliminate it. Reducing the number of choices can make the question more manageable.
- **Cover Up the Answers**: Try reading the question and predicting the answer before looking at the options. Then uncover the options and see if any match your prediction.
- **Look for Absolute Words**: Be cautious with options that contain words like "always," "never," or "only." Such absolutes are not common in the flexible and diverse field of nursing.
- **Watch Out for Similar Options**: If two options seem very similar, they are likely either both correct or both incorrect. Compare them closely to determine their validity.
- **Consider Your Nursing Knowledge**: Apply your foundational nursing knowledge. If an option goes against basic nursing principles, it's likely incorrect.
- **Practice Makes Perfect**: Regularly practice with SATA questions to get comfortable with the format. The more you practice, the more intuitive your approach will become.
- **Stay Calm and Focused**: SATA questions can be intimidating. Approach them calmly and methodically to avoid feeling overwhelmed.
- **Review All Options Before Finalizing**: Even if you find one true statement, review all others. There could be multiple correct answers.
- **Don't Overthink**: It's easy to over-analyze and doubt your choices in SATA questions. Trust your training and first instincts unless you find clear evidence to change your answer.
- **Beware of Changing Answers**: Avoid changing your answers unless you have a strong reason to do so. Often, your first choice is the correct one.
- **Use NCLEX Study Resources**: Utilize NCLEX study guides and practice questions specifically designed for SATA to hone your skills.

Critical Thinking and Clinical Judgment

- Mastering critical thinking and clinical judgment is crucial for success in the NCLEX-RN exam, as well as in your future nursing practice. These skills enable you to make sound decisions in complex clinical situations.
- **Understand the Nursing Process**: Familiarize yourself with the steps of the nursing process (assessment, diagnosis, planning, implementation, and evaluation). This structured approach is fundamental to critical thinking in nursing.
- **Practice Scenario-Based Questions**: Engage with practice questions that mimic real-life scenarios. This will help you apply theoretical knowledge to practical situations, a key aspect of clinical judgment.
- **Analyze, Don't Just Memorize**: While memorizing facts is important, the NCLEX-RN focuses on your ability to analyze information and make decisions. Always ask yourself 'why' when studying different conditions and treatments.
- **Enhance Your Prioritization Skills**: Practice determining which patient problems require immediate attention and which can wait. Prioritization is a crucial part of clinical judgment.
- **Reflect on Clinical Experiences**: If you have clinical experience, reflect on the cases you've encountered. Think about what went well, what could have been done differently, and how theory applies to practice.
- **Develop a Systematic Approach**: Develop a methodical approach to answering questions. Start by understanding what the question is asking, then systematically evaluate each option.
- **Break Down Complex Questions**: Learn to dissect complex questions into smaller, more manageable parts to better understand what is being asked.
- **Stay Informed About Best Practices**: Keep up-to-date with current best practices, guidelines, and research findings in nursing. This knowledge base is crucial for making informed clinical decisions.
- **Practice 'Thinking Aloud'**: When studying, articulate your thought process. This can help clarify your thinking and reveal areas where you

need more understanding.
- **Seek Varied Learning Experiences**: Exposure to different clinical situations, whether through simulations, case studies, or clinical rotations, can enhance your ability to think critically and make sound judgments.
- **Consult with Peers and Mentors**: Discussing clinical scenarios and NCLEX-style questions with peers or mentors can expose you to different viewpoints and reasoning strategies.
- **Learn from Mistakes**: When you get a practice question wrong, take time to understand why. This reflection can greatly enhance your critical thinking abilities.
- **Stay Calm Under Pressure**: Developing the ability to stay calm and think clearly under pressure is key. Practice stress-reduction techniques that work for you.
- **Embrace Lifelong Learning**: Critical thinking and clinical judgment are skills that continue to develop throughout your nursing career. Stay curious and open to learning.

Time Management During the Exam

- Effective time management is a key component for success in the NCLEX-RN exam. Managing your time efficiently can help you navigate through questions calmly and thoroughly.
- **Understand the Timing Structure**: Know that you have up to 6 hours to complete the exam, including any optional breaks. This includes time for the tutorial, sample items, and any unscheduled breaks you might take.
- **Start with a Steady Pace**: Begin the exam at a consistent pace. Aim to spend approximately one minute per question. This will help you get into a rhythm and prevent rushing through questions.
- **Monitor Your Progress**: Periodically check the time to ensure you're not falling behind. However, avoid constantly watching the clock as it can increase anxiety.
- **Use the Tutorial Wisely**: Utilize the tutorial time to familiarize yourself with the format and navigation of the exam. This can save you time

during the actual test.
- **Prioritize Questions Appropriately**: Spend more time on questions that require critical thinking and less on those that are straightforward or based on recall.
- **Don't Get Stuck on Difficult Questions**: If you find yourself stuck, make the best educated guess and move on. Remember, you can't return to previous questions, so dwelling too long on one question can eat into your time for others.
- **Plan Your Breaks Strategically**: You are allowed to take breaks, but the exam clock will continue to run. Plan to take short breaks only if necessary, to refresh and refocus.
- **Practice Time Management in Prep Tests**: During your preparation, practice full-length tests under timed conditions to get a feel for the pace you need to maintain.
- **Be Prepared for the Length**: Be mentally prepared for both a shorter and a longer test, as the NCLEX can end anytime after the minimum number of questions (75).
- **Avoid Rushing Through the Last Questions**: If you find yourself nearing the end of the allowed time, try not to rush. Hasty answers can lead to mistakes.
- **Keep a Clear Mind**: A calm and clear mind can think and process information faster. Practice relaxation techniques that work for you to maintain composure during the exam.
- **Use Elimination to Save Time**: For multiple-choice questions, quickly eliminate obviously incorrect answers to streamline your decision-making process.
- **Read Each Question Carefully**: While you want to maintain a steady pace, ensure you read each question carefully. Misreading a question can lead to an incorrect answer, wasting the time you spent on it.
- **Stay Hydrated and Energized**: Take care of your physical well-being. Staying hydrated and having a good meal before the exam can help maintain your energy levels and concentration.

Stress Reduction and Anxiety Management

- Remember that some level of stress is normal when taking a high-stakes exam like the NCLEX. It's how you manage and channel that stress that makes a difference.
- **Practice Mindfulness Meditation**: Incorporate mindfulness meditation into your daily routine. This practice can help you stay present, reduce anxiety, and improve concentration. Apps and guided sessions are readily available to assist you.
- **Exercise Regularly**: Engaging in regular physical activity can help reduce stress and anxiety. Even short, daily walks can make a significant difference in your overall well-being.
- **Create a Study Schedule**: Organize your study time efficiently. Create a study schedule that includes breaks and adheres to your body's natural rhythms. Adequate sleep is essential, so ensure you get enough rest.
- **Use Relaxation Techniques**: Learn relaxation techniques such as deep breathing exercises, progressive muscle relaxation, or guided imagery. These methods can help you stay calm during the exam.
- **Healthy Diet**: Maintain a balanced diet with plenty of fruits, vegetables, and whole grains. Avoid excessive caffeine intake, as it can increase anxiety. Stay hydrated to keep your brain functioning optimally.
- **Practice Test-Taking Strategies**: Familiarize yourself with test-taking strategies specific to the NCLEX. Learn how to break down questions, eliminate incorrect options, and choose the best answer based on your nursing knowledge.
- **Review Regularly**: Consistent review of nursing content is crucial. Use reputable NCLEX review books, apps, and practice exams to reinforce your knowledge and build confidence.
- **Seek Support**: Don't hesitate to reach out to classmates, professors, or a support network when you feel overwhelmed. Discussing your concerns and sharing experiences can be comforting.
- **Simulate Exam Conditions**: Take practice exams under simulated test conditions. Time yourself, and try to mimic the environment of the actual

NCLEX exam. This will help reduce test-day anxiety.
- **Stay Positive**: Maintain a positive mindset. Believe in your preparation and abilities. Negative thoughts can increase stress, so practice positive self-talk.
- **Utilize Relaxation Techniques Before the Exam**: Before entering the testing center, take a few moments to perform relaxation techniques. Deep breathing or visualization exercises can help calm your nerves.
- **Stay Informed**: Familiarize yourself with the logistics of the NCLEX exam day, including the testing center's location, parking, identification requirements, and scheduling details. Being well-prepared can reduce pre-test anxiety.

Review and Practice Questions

- Remember that NCLEX success comes from a combination of knowledge, critical thinking skills, and effective test-taking strategies.
- **Start Early**: Begin your review and practice questions well in advance of your scheduled exam date. Spreading your preparation over several weeks or months can help you retain information better than cramming.
- **Create a Study Plan**: Develop a structured study plan that outlines what topics you'll cover each day or week. Allocate specific time for review and practice questions in your daily schedule.
- **Use NCLEX Review Materials**: Invest in reputable NCLEX review materials, such as review books, online courses, or mobile apps. These resources are tailored to the exam's content and format.
- **Focus on Weak Areas**: Identify your areas of weakness and prioritize them during your review. Spend more time on topics where you feel less confident.
- **Practice Daily**: Dedicate time each day to practice questions. Consistency is key to improving your test-taking skills and knowledge retention.
- **Mix Question Types**: Practice a variety of question types, including multiple-choice, select-all-that-apply (SATA), and prioritization questions. This helps you become familiar with the NCLEX question format.

- **Simulate Exam Conditions**: Take practice tests under exam-like conditions. Time yourself, avoid distractions, and use the same level of concentration as you would on test day.
- **Review Rationales**: After answering practice questions, review the rationales for both correct and incorrect answers. Understanding why an answer is correct or incorrect is crucial for learning.
- **Learn From Mistakes**: Don't get discouraged by incorrect answers. Instead, use them as learning opportunities. Analyze your mistakes, understand the underlying concepts, and strive not to repeat them.
- **Use Flashcards**: Create flashcards for key concepts, medications, lab values, and nursing interventions. Flashcards are an effective way to reinforce memorization.
- **Study in Groups**: Consider joining or forming a study group with fellow nursing students. Discussing questions and sharing insights can enhance your understanding.
- **Take Breaks**: Avoid burnout by taking regular breaks during your study sessions. Short, frequent breaks can improve your focus and retention.
- **Practice Time Management**: During the actual exam, you'll need to manage your time wisely. Practice pacing yourself when answering questions to ensure you have enough time for the entire test.
- **Read Questions Carefully**: Pay close attention to the wording of each question. NCLEX questions can be tricky, and understanding what is being asked is crucial.
- **Stay Positive**: Maintain a positive attitude throughout your preparation. A positive mindset can boost your confidence and performance on test day.
- **Stay Healthy**: Eat nutritious meals, exercise regularly, and get enough sleep. A healthy body and mind are better equipped to handle the rigors of NCLEX preparation.
- **Simulate Exam Day**: Prior to the actual exam, do a trial run to the testing center. This will help you familiarize yourself with the location and reduce anxiety on the day of the test.

Continuing Education and Lifelong Learning

- Continuing education and lifelong learning are cornerstones of a successful nursing career. They not only enhance your knowledge and skills but also ensure that you provide the best possible care to your patients throughout your career.
- **Embrace Lifelong Learning**: Nursing is a dynamic field with ever-evolving knowledge and technologies. Commit to a lifelong journey of learning and professional growth.
- **Stay Informed**: Keep up with the latest developments in nursing by reading nursing journals, attending conferences, and following reputable nursing websites and social media channels.
- **Engage in Continuing Education**: Pursue continuing education opportunities, such as workshops, webinars, and online courses, to expand your knowledge and skills. Many of these activities offer continuing education units (CEUs) to maintain your licensure.
- **Join Professional Associations**: Consider joining nursing organizations related to your area of interest. These associations often provide access to resources, networking opportunities, and educational events.
- **Seek Mentorship**: Connect with experienced nurses who can serve as mentors. They can offer guidance, share their expertise, and provide valuable insights into your nursing career.
- **Set Learning Goals**: Establish clear learning goals and objectives for yourself. This helps you stay focused and motivated on your educational journey.
- **Explore Specializations**: Nursing offers a wide range of specializations. Explore different areas of nursing to discover where your passion lies. Specializing can lead to more focused and rewarding career opportunities.
- **Utilize Online Resources**: Take advantage of online platforms and e-learning resources. Many universities and organizations offer free or affordable online courses and materials.
- **Stay Current with Guidelines**: Familiarize yourself with nursing practice guidelines and standards, such as those from the American Nurses Asso-

ciation (ANA) and specialty organizations. Adhering to these guidelines is essential for quality care.
- **Network with Peers**: Connect with fellow nursing students and professionals. Networking can lead to valuable collaborations, information exchange, and support.
- **Attend Conferences**: Whenever possible, attend nursing conferences and symposiums. These events provide opportunities to learn from experts, explore new research, and network with colleagues.
- **Practice Reflective Learning**: Regularly reflect on your clinical experiences and patient interactions. Analyze what went well and what could be improved. Reflective practice enhances your critical thinking and decision-making skills.
- **Stay Ethical and Legal**: Keep yourself updated on ethical and legal issues in nursing practice. Understanding your professional responsibilities and legal obligations is crucial.
- **Balance Work and Learning**: Striking a balance between your nursing career and ongoing education is essential. Plan your learning activities around your work schedule to avoid burnout.
- **Celebrate Achievements**: Acknowledge and celebrate your educational milestones and achievements. Recognizing your progress can boost your motivation to continue learning.
- **Stay Curious**: Cultivate curiosity and a thirst for knowledge. Ask questions, seek answers, and explore new areas of interest within the nursing profession.
- **Remember the Impact**: Always keep in mind the positive impact your continued education and commitment to lifelong learning can have on patient care and the nursing profession as a whole.

12

Claim Your Bonus Guide Here and Leave a Review:

BONUS: Complementary Study Guide Downloadable

Are you aiming to master the complexities of pharmacology? Looking for a quick and handy reference? We've got just the thing for you!

🌟 Get Your Exclusive FREE NCLEX Study Guide! 🌟

With every purchase, we're offering a downloadable and printable NCLEX Study Guide, tailored specially for the dedicated nurse in you. Imagine having a concise, organized, and efficient sheet right at your fingertips, perfect for those quick glances and last-minute revisions.

💡 Why Should You Claim Your Study Guide?

Save Time: No more rummaging through notes. Get answers quickly.
 Enhance Knowledge: Brush up on vital NCLEX information in no time.
 Portable: Printed or digital, take it wherever you go.
 Exclusive Offer: This cheat sheet is designed uniquely for our community.

Absolutely FREE: Because we value and appreciate your dedication.

So, whether you're a seasoned nurse looking to brush up your knowledge or a nursing student preparing for your exams, this cheat sheet is an invaluable addition to your resources.

🎁 Claim Your Free NCLEX Study Guide Now! 🎁

It's not just a purchase; it's an investment in your nursing career.

Claim it here: https://oasisninja.com/nclex

Elevate your nursing game. Equip yourself with the best tools. You've got this! 💪💖

Again, claim it here: https://oasisninja.com/nclex/

Leave a Review!

Hey Amazing Readers! 📖✨

Did you recently dive into "NCLEX RN Review Simplified"? If so, we'd love to hear your thoughts!

🌟 *Why Your Review Matters:* 🌟

- **Share Your Insight**: Help fellow nurses and students by sharing your personal takeaways.
- **Community Building**: Your feedback contributes to a community of passionate learners, all aiming to elevate their nursing knowledge.
- **Continuous Improvement**: By sharing your perspective, you help us enhance future editions and resources.

📖 **How to Leave Your Review:**

CLAIM YOUR BONUS GUIDE HERE AND LEAVE A REVIEW:

It's super easy and takes just a few minutes!

1. Click on this Link to navigate to Amazon review section of this book.
2. Pick a star rating from 1 to 5 (5 being the best). And share your thoughts, whether they're about the book's structure, the clarity of explanations, or the real-world applications you've found beneficial.

And there's more!

Every review is a chance for us to better serve our readers and the broader nursing community.

So, if "NCLEX RN Review Simplified" has made a difference in your studies or practice, please take a moment to let us and the world know.

Drop Your Review Here: https://www.amazon.com/review/create-review/?ie=UTF8&channel=glance-detail&asin=B0CP4BZJ1F

Your voice matters, and together, we can make the world of nursing education even better. Thank you for your dedication, and for being an integral part of our community!

Again, click here to leave a review for this book or go to the link above!

Afterword

References

Billings, D. M., & Hensel, D. (2021). Lippincott Q&A Review for NCLEX-RN. Wolters Kluwer Health.

Davis, L. A. (2020). Davis's Q&A Review for NCLEX-RN. F.A. Davis Company.

Hargrove-Huttel, R. A., & Colgrove, K. A. (2019). Mosby's Comprehensive Review of Nursing for NCLEX-RN. Elsevier.

Hogan, M. A., & Unverzagt, J. (2020). NCLEX-RN Review Guide: Top Ten Questions for Quick Review. Jones & Bartlett Learning.

Kaplan Nursing. (2021). NCLEX-RN Prep Plus. Kaplan Publishing.

LaCharity, L. A., Kumagai, C. K., & Bartz, B. (2021). Prioritization, Delegation, and Assignment: Practice Exercises for the NCLEX Examination. Elsevier.

Lisko, S. A. (2019). Saunders Comprehensive Review for the NCLEX-RN Examination. Elsevier.

Ohman, K. (2019). NCLEX-RN Secrets Study Guide: Your Key to Exam Success. Mometrix Media LLC.

Silvestri, L. A., & Silvestri, A. E. (2020). Saunders Strategies for Test Success:

Passing Nursing School and the NCLEX Exam. Elsevier.

Silvestri, L. A. (2021). Saunders Q&A Review for the NCLEX-RN Examination. Elsevier.

Sloan, R., & Hurd, A. (2020). Adult CCRN/PCCN Certification Review: Think in Questions, Learn by Rationale. Springer Publishing Company.

Spurlock, D. R. (2019). NCLEX-RN 101: How to Pass!. Springer Publishing Company.

Swearingen, P. L. (2019). All-In-One Care Planning Resource. Elsevier.

Synder, M. (2021). Illustrated Study Guide for the NCLEX-RN Exam. Elsevier.

Vallerand, A. H., & Sanoski, C. A. (2019). Davis's Drug Guide for Nurses. F.A. Davis Company.

Warner, R. (2021). NCLEX-RN Content Review Guide. Kaplan Publishing.

Wilda, R. (2020). NCLEX-RN Drug Guide: 300 Medications You Need to Know for the Exam. Kaplan Publishing.

Zerwekh, J., & Garneau, A. Z. (2021). Memory Notebook of Nursing. Nursing Education Consultants.

Zerwekh, J. (2020). Nursing Today: Transition and Trends. Elsevier.

Zurakowski, T. L., & Snyder, C. L. (2019). NCLEX-RN Review Made Incredibly Easy!. Wolters Kluwer Health.

About the Author

Mark Aquino RN

Mark Aquino is a registered nurse in California with a Bachelors of Science in Nursing and Masters of Health Administration from West Coast University. He has at least 4 years of experience in the front lines as a visiting nurse in home health and hospice care, and counting, as he still continues to see patients at the time of this writing. He is author of OASIS NINJA: A Home Health Nurse's Guide to Visits, Documentation, and Positive Patient Outcomes. This guide provides nurses with the information they need to provide quality care to their patients in the comfort of their own homes. He also writes books about how to live a good life and how to improve yourself on a daily basis. Learn more at OasisNinja.com.

—

Check out more books by this author at OasisNinja.com - https://oasisninja.com

Made in the USA
Las Vegas, NV
06 March 2024